T0029109

ON PURPOSE

ON PURPOSE

Ten Lessons on the Meaning of Life

BEN HUTCHINSON

4th ESTATE • *London*

4th Estate
An imprint of HarperCollins*Publishers*
1 London Bridge Street
London SE1 9GF

www.4thEstate.co.uk

HarperCollins*Publishers*
Macken House
39/40 Mayor Street Upper
Dublin 1 D01 C9W8
Ireland

First published in Great Britain in 2023 by 4th Estate

1

Set in Adobe Garamond Pro

Printed and bound in the UK using 100% renewable electricity
at CPI Group (UK) Ltd

This book is produced from independently certified FSC™ paper
to ensure responsible forest management

For more information visit: www.harpercollins.co.uk/green

*'To live is the rarest thing in the world.
Most people exist, that is all.'*

OSCAR WILDE

CONTENTS

PROLOGUE

I LEARNED HOW TO LIVE, which is to say I learned how to read, around the turn of the millennium. The world was young, Labour was 'new', and I was just getting going. Until my early twenties, it had all been about the path of least persistence, about maximum coasting at minimum cost. Contemporaries with career paths, into law and finance, into the industries of the educated, baffled me; not because I disapproved of their choices, but because I could not muster their motivation. Concentration was beyond me, an arena of ambition that I had yet even to imagine, let alone enter. Like characters in a play by Samuel Beckett – drift and drag, wallow and wander – my defining verbs were not so much doing words as stalling words, modes of waiting in a mud of stasis. Nothing much was happening, repeatedly. When would life begin in earnest?

The answer, it turned out, was when I started reading in earnest. Sometime in the late 1990s I had an epiphany: words are what give us meaning. The trick, I began to realise, was to take this literally. I'd studied languages, I'd learned the rules;

I knew the semantics of sense and signification. But I hadn't twigged that meaning is also *meaning*, that language, used artfully, points to purpose. Not just that of others, but also, it now hit me, my own. Words, ideas, the life of the mind: here was a way not just to live, but to come alive.

The path ahead of me beckoned. Language, I was starting to see, does not just help us communicate and cogitate – it opens up unparalleled worlds of history and culture, parallel worlds of insight and understanding. A book is *un livre* is *ein Buch* is *un libro*. They are all the same, but they are all different, variously imagined in various cultures. In the interstices between them, in the ways in which words are used not just to connect but to create, direction dawned. Culture is comparative, greater than any of us – and so, I was beginning to realise, is meaning. It was as though I'd put on headphones with simultaneous translation, interpreting the world into perfect clarity. Suddenly, I understood the world and my modest place in it. I had found my voice.

'All I have is a voice', writes W.H. Auden. In the end, that is all any of us has, the tiniest of tremors in a universe of indifference. But we can train it, like a singer; we can tune it, like a writer; we can tutor it, like a reader. Used well, our voice can echo in millions of heads. If we remember in particular the line that follows Auden's claim – 'we must love one another or die' – it's because we respond not just to the sentiment but to the simplicity, to the common contours of the human condition. Auden himself found the line glib, 'infected with an incurable dishonesty'. Despite his misgivings, his voice has moved millions of readers, as though sheer strength of feeling could forestall the inevitability of death.

Death may be inevitable, but living is not, at least not in its enhanced, existential sense. My quarter-life crisis taught me this much: we have to work out what we want to do with our lives. We have to find our voice. As we grow older and settle into maturity, we start to intuit the finitude of things, including our own existence and its limited number of possibilities. We are what we articulate, if only to ourselves. Our self-image is our self-imagination. Until my early twenties, my internal narrative had been one of circumstance and complacency. With the leap into maturity, it became one of substance and curiosity. The headphones of culture tuned out the noise and forced me to focus.

We can all learn to focus. To live fully, we have to hear fully: words give meaning to life because they give *voice* to the meaning of life. We can choose to couch this impulse in religious terms – 'Glory be to God for dappled things' – but really there is no need: poets are secular prophets. 'Praise *this* world, not the untold world', writes the great Austrian poet Rainer Maria Rilke in his ninth Duino Elegy (1922). It is enough – it is *hard* enough – to acknowledge what is in front of us.

To a greater or lesser extent, all writing testifies to this simple truth. We can't predict the future. We can't call up certainty. We can, however, inject ourselves with insight; we can inhale imagination. All we have to do is pick up a book. All we have to do is read – not just because we learn from or through books, but because the very existence of literature, as a form of art predicated on the use of words to express ideas or identities, presupposes the possibility of meaning. If the test of a true book is whether it functions as an axe for the frozen sea inside us – to develop, once more, Franz Kafka's over-exposed aphorism – this implies that we have an internal sea in the first place, and that it is worth exploring.

For many of us, and certainly for me, it is our feelings that are frozen as much as our minds. Wary of emotion, suspicious of sentiment, I took refuge, as I emerged unready into adulthood, in dispassionate scholarship, in 'the life of the mind'. What I hadn't yet realised was that the *life* of the mind is something else again, more elusive and mercurial, more conditional on figuring out why it is that we spend so much time living it in the first place. I hadn't yet realised that meaning requires attention, like a long-term relationship that has been taken for granted. The meaning of our lives *is* our longest-term relationship, and we do take it for granted.

Art, if we only listen, shows us this all along. Weirder and more disturbing than it first sounds, Kafka's celebrated statement makes the point memorably when put back into its original context: 'I think we ought to read only the kind of books that wound and stab us. If the book we're reading doesn't wake us up with a blow on the head, what are we reading it for? [. . .] We need the books that affect us like a disaster, that grieve us deeply, like the death of someone we loved more than ourselves, like being banished into forests far from anyone, like a suicide. A book must be the axe for the frozen sea inside us.' A motivational speech this is not.

What it is, though, is a love letter, among the darkest ever written, to the power of literature. Reading and writing are professions of faith in the possibility of purpose: why else do we turn to books if not to broaden our sense of the capacities of life? In their very existence, in the very energy involved in writing them, all books are life-affirming, even those that would seek to deny or denigrate life, to banish us into forests far from anyone. The most nihilistic of works is still a creative act, powered by purpose.

This book itemises such purpose. Identifying ten lessons from literature for the meaning – and meanness – of life, it explores the ways in which reading and writing can help us ask difficult questions, challenge the status quo, project our minds into the past and future, imagine other worlds, and see ourselves and others differently. The impact of literature, the force of the word, cannot be stated strongly enough: in the secular universe of post-Enlightenment modernity, writing has shaped us as much as any army or religion. The way we think of our personal identities, to take just one example, is nothing if not post-Romantic. The way we think of our professional careers is nothing if not post-Realistic; all of us are the protagonists of our own *Bildungsroman*. What, though, is the precise strength of literature as a moral force? How can it teach us to lead fuller, richer lives? And how can it help give us that elusive sense of meaning?

'Meaning', like 'cool', is one of those great abstract nouns we spend much of our lives pursuing without ever quite knowing what they are. Quarantined in quotation marks they retreat as we advance, recoiling from our attempts to understand them. It's always been said that you can't be cool if you have to ask what it is. Perhaps meaning is the opposite, in that it can *only* be obtained by asking what it is. We can't judge our own coolness, but we can and must judge our own meaning. To reflect on purpose is to live on purpose: the grammar of meaning is nothing if not self-conscious, a deliberation on how to live deliberately. There must be a user's manual somewhere. There must be a map.

Literature has always been my map – not in the physical sense of charting coordinates, but in the metaphysical sense of indicating direction. Here be meaning: even a blank page points to purpose, to the cartography of consciousness. It starts, of course, with children's literature, which plays a vital role in how we develop as autonomous agents. Our sense of ourselves and our place in society, our moral and emotional capacities, are established early on in life by the formative stories that we encounter when young. It is not so much the content or plot of these stories that shape us – all those quest narratives and escapist fantasies, all those plucky little outsiders who take on the dull, unimaginative grown-ups – as their tone or voice, the vivid charm of an A.A. Milne or the morbid cruelty of a Roald Dahl. The hand that writes the fable writes the world.

As we grow older we seek independence, which means

that we seek a greater intensity of experience. Ambushed by adolescence, we begin, at first tentatively and then urgently to establish our own autonomous identity. We 'rebel'. Our sense of self is keyed not only to its outward manifestations – to the long hair and earrings, to the carefully curated T-shirts – but to its inward pressures, to the egotistical sublime of the teenage mind. We speak of reading 'voraciously', an adverb that suggests not so much satisfaction as *dis*satisfaction, a melancholy awareness that we can never ingest sufficient narrative momentum. Can we *mean* voraciously? Can we *be* voraciously? Such is the adolescent ambition.

It's far from certain, though, that it makes us happy. If we think of the most voracious moments in our lives – particularly our younger lives – they tend to be moments of self-forgetting. Sex, drugs and rock 'n' roll: the cliché is of unconsciousness, an unholy trinity of self-suppression. Yet we can't live at a constant pitch of intensity; mere oblivion, by definition, won't clarify consciousness. Happiness cannot just be climax, or the rest of life will be anti-climax. We have to find ways of bringing meaning out of the privileged moment and into life as a whole.

This is where literature can help. 'We live entirely [. . .] by the imposition of a narrative line upon disparate images', wrote Joan Didion in 1979, proving her point by corralling assorted offcuts of the Californian surreal. Our moods, our identity and self-esteem, depend on our constantly shifting responses to external stimuli, to the many microaggressions of the everyday. The sea can make me feel sad or exhilarated, friends can make me feel empowered or emasculated. It depends on how I read them. It depends on my narrative line.

Another way of saying this is that my view of life depends on how I edit life. My coy ellipsis in Didion's statement gives the game away: we live entirely, *especially if we are writers*, by the imposition of a narrative line. 'Especially', but not exclusively, since we all seek to impose meaning of some sort on those unruly images. Prisoners of our perspectives, we are also the editors of existence, giving rhythm and cadence, rise and fall, to the parameters of our life sentence. Perhaps we just need to think about life as though we were writing it.

Writing – drafting, reading, deleting and redrafting – transcends the prison of the present. It places us not just in time, but out of time. Like Proust with his scallop-shaped madeleine, words help us make the pilgrimage to the past. But they also help us look to the future. In his 'Defence of Poetry' (1821), Percy Bysshe Shelley casts poets not only as the guardians of the 'spirit of the age', but as the guarantors of posterity. Importantly, however, they themselves do not consciously agitate for any particular cause. They have 'little apparent correspondence with that spirit of good of which they are the ministers', but serve merely as conductors of the 'electric life which burns within their words'. It is their disinterest that guarantees their interest, their distance from the present that means they can legislate for the future. 'Poets are the hierophants of an unapprehended inspiration,' writes Shelley in his celebrated conclusion, 'the mirrors of the gigantic shadows which futurity casts upon the present; the words which express what they understand not; the trumpets which sing to battle, and feel not what they inspire; the influence which is moved not, but moves. Poets are the unacknowledged legislators of the world.'

Is it time we acknowledged them? If we take the idea of legislation not as a legal or political term but as a moral or emotional one, it becomes possible to understand poets – and writers more generally – as the unacknowledged legislators of meaning. Writers, I want to suggest, are the prophets of purpose. Whenever we are unsure of ourselves or our place on the planet, we can turn to literature for alternative existences, alternative articulations of how and why we get out of bed in the morning. While none of us knows for sure the meaning of life, the hive mind of literary history comes as close as anyone to disclosing it. The democracy of the dead, to yoke Chesterton to Churchill, is the worst form of government except all the others that have been tried. Our ten commandments should come not from the Book, in short, but from books: a decalogue for our daily struggle.

WHAT DOES this struggle feel like? What does it mean to live meaningfully?

Covid made us reassess many things, like a quarter-life crisis for the twenty-first century. One of the most basic questions it raised is not just what we want from life, but how we managed to avoid asking the question in the first place.

So many of us drift into jobs, relationships and ways of living just because they are there, without ever really taking the time to stand back and work out whether we want them. Things happen to us, because something has to; *making* things happen – and the sense that this even matters – escapes us with the years. Active choices become passive non-choices.

Lockdown locked us up – the coy prepositional shift not-withstanding – but it also unlocked a reservoir of questions. Do we want to keep drifting through life, allowing things to happen *to* us? Do we want to keep doing things the way we did before? Or is it time to reassess not just what we wish for, but the very idea of wishing *for* something? Can we live, can we think, on purpose?

Purpose is provisional, this much is clear. As we move through Shakespeare's seven ages, we do not pursue the same goals as our earlier incarnations. The soldier 'seeking the bubble reputation' becomes the justice 'full of wise saws and modern instances'. Sans everything, we are also, in the end, sans ambition: nothing more is to be gained in second child-ishness. Like life itself, purpose outpaces us. We do not attain it, and retain it, once and for all; there is no lifetime guarantee of meaning. It is more like a constant flickering of focus, a constant re-tuning of the radio.

Some mornings I wake up fully charged, an iPad gleam-ing green on 100 per cent, a vivid sense of purpose pulsing through me. The air crackles with electricity as I sip my coffee, zipping together the dots of the day ahead. The clarity of focus tastes almost bitter, like the caffeine: sharp, approaching painful, just a little too hot for the tip of my tongue. Wake up, it warns me; watch out. Something is beginning.

Other mornings, I may as well not have bothered. The day is dull, drawn, devoid of promise, grey thoughts under grey skies. Static, woolly, unresponsive, I sit in the kitchen incapable of clarity. The air tastes soupy, indiscriminate, the coffee can do nothing to console me. The crackle – this much is certain – will not cohere.

We are all familiar with versions of these feelings. Focus is ephemeral, concentration fleeting. In the attention economy of our lives, we are perennially overdrawn and underinvested. Between drift and drive, apathy and energy, all too often we tend to the former, to the art of least resistance. What, though, if there were a way to train our attention, to capture our gaze? What if we could learn to compel our fugitive thoughts?

Reading is one way of doing this, as numerous neuroscientific studies have demonstrated. But really, we don't need brain scans to know as much: any child with her nose in Harry Potter could tell us. Drawn in by the characters, drawn on by the plot, we are self-sufficient for the duration of the story. Within the boundaries of the book, life has meaning – it has meaning because we *give* it meaning. Burrowed in words, borrowed from words, we find a form of purpose.

Such purpose, I have come to realise, is as powerful as any drug. I'd go so far as to say, in fact, that literature *is* a drug, with all the ambivalence this implies: it liberates and anaesthetises us, it vivifies and narcotises us. Ever since antiquity, literature has been both malady and cure, remedy and poison, the double-edged *pharmakon* of Platonic fame. The tease of meaning is just another line away. Above all, of course, this makes reading and writing addictive, drawing us in with the promise of ever-greater knowledge, ever-greater insight into our human perdition. In my own life, literature literally took the place of drugs. There was considerable overlap – many months of marijuana, many months of reading – but looking back now I see that even in those lost years of late adolescence, images and ideas were slowly supplanting pills and powder as my principal source of stimulation. Like my ellipsis [. . .] in Didion's narrative line, the emptiness had meaning, if only the gradual realisation that the imagination is its own best intoxicant. Dante pops off the page when stoned, no doubt about it, but Hell is pretty hallucinatory even without the help. Baudelaire hardly needed his hash cakes to revolutionise modern poetry, nor Virginia Woolf her chloral – 'that mighty prince with the moth's eyes and feathered feet' – to revolutionise modern prose. And the less said about the Beat poets, the better.

Little by little, weed gave way to words as I slouched towards maturity, pupils dilating with the promise of subtler purpose. Framed in these terms it even sounds like a drug, like one of those terrible names they give to strains of LSD: Pink Floyd, Flying Saucer, Subtler Purpose. Meaning, I was starting to realise, could be repackaged in more capacious, more variable terms as not just about me and my own febrile state of mind, not just a passing moment of pleasure. That

I could learn from others in a serious and sustained way, that this could be a lifelong project of growth and discovery beyond adolescent indolence: was my exit strategy from the narcissism of youth. That age-old question of childhood – what do you want to be when you grow up? – suddenly had an answer. I grew up.

When I first conceived this book, I was thinking about a very simple question: how would I justify my life to my children? What advice would I give to them on the basis of my adult experience? Twelve- and ten-year-old boys don't always read as much as they might, but they do ask disarmingly direct questions. What's the point of life? What's the point of reading? What's the point of anything? Literature no more has final answers to such questions than anyone else, but what it does offer is an alphabet for their articulation. The ABC of meaning, if such a thing existed, would necessarily entail words, and words find their fullest exposition in literary writing. We are what we read.

But what, and why, *do* we read? What, in Milton's words, is 'the benefit which may be had of books promiscuously read'? Why, in my own words, have I dedicated my life to literature? The answer, I think, is that at a crucial stage in my development I was drawn to writing as a mechanism for meaning, for a sense of subtlety, beauty – and yes, difficulty – beyond everyday discourse. Why make small talk, I thought to myself, when you can read great books? Why smoke second-rate hash when you can read first-rate writing? Beyond the fog, behind the chit-chat, lie ghostlier demarcations, keener sounds. Hopelessly idealistic, to be sure, not to men-tion hopelessly insulting to the many subtle, beautiful and difficult people who have enriched my everyday discourse. Even in maturity, though, something of the earnest glamour, the adolescent overreach, still obtains.

Mature critics, like mature parents, legislate the param-eters of meaning. Why privilege one text over another? Why choose this experience over that one? Such questions apply to life just as they apply to literature. The throb of self-doubt, the ache and anxiety that we feel when contemplating our uncer-tain future on an uncertain planet, are the very essence of art: its pointlessness is its point. In existence as in aesthetics, there is no cure for contingency. Exiled from Eden, condemned to consciousness, we have such meaning as we ascribe.

The lessons explored in this book might also, of course, be learned from other sources. History teaches, it just has no pupils, to paraphrase the Austrian poet Ingeborg Bachmann. But it is the privilege of literature to invoke the imagination as both a moral and a discursive force. To put it more simply: literature can both *exemplify* and *examine* how to live; it can both describe a story and dissect it. It can make us feel, as well as think.

All literature can do this, but we have to start from some-where, from what we know. As Virginia Woolf wrote in 1925, 'the mind takes its bias from the place of its birth'. In the case of Western readers, this bias is towards Western litera-ture, however problematic its history and politics. But then confronting such problems is part of why we read, part of the challenge that the humanities pose to us – the core question of which is that of meaning. To reflect on the purpose of the humanities is to reflect on the purpose of life, since both of them resist reduction.

Reading, like living, is its own reward, since it pushes us beyond the many instrumental necessities – travelling to work, caring for children, doing the shopping – of our hurried, harried lives. Reading, like living, is precisely *not* instrumental, which is what makes it so valuable. It is not so much a safe space as a stray space, yet to be colonised by capitalism. If the humanities increasingly feel the need to justify themselves through recourse to another discipline (sub-dividing into areas such as medical, digital or environmental humanities), the adjectives miss the point, which is that humanism – promiscuous reading – is not supposed to have a pre-packaged orientation or message. For neither, of course, do humans.

As an essayist and critic, I have long believed in the edifying powers of 'great writing'. In truth, though, this belief, in strikingly non-Socratic manner, has long lain unexamined. In reducing it to ten precepts, in capturing it in ten commandments, I am attempting to hold my vague humanist credo up to the light, and in doing so to convey the power of literature to power our lives. Such is the aim of this album of essays: ten songs in praise of purpose.

It is for each of us to decide what kind of purpose. Just as we all differ in our tastes and experiences, so we all differ in the degree of emphasis that we afford our life ambitions.

Some of us prioritise self-fulfilment, others prefer self-suppression. Some of us seek identity and community, others flee them. We each have different demons, and different desires. What matters to us all, however, is that we find some form of purpose, even – or especially – if such purpose is itself, ultimately, a figment of the imagination. In our godless age, meaning may be a mirage – perhaps even a MacGuffin, in Hitchcock's sense of something that exists simply to get the story going. But it is necessary all the same. Life may be accidental, but living should not be; without some sense of direction drawing us over the horizon, we are just drifting aimlessly across the desert of life. This, then, is what I say to my sons, and to anyone else who is wondering how to be – or become – a meaningful person, a person *full of meaning*: live, read and reflect on purpose.

I

Think of all the beauty around you and be happy

Lesson one: Pursue pleasure in the knowledge that it is transient

THE FIRST DUTY that we have to life is to enjoy it. I want to be happy, you want to be happy, who doesn't want to be happy? Even in the most scandalous of circumstances, even in the most untenable of situations, we seek fulfilment where we can. Albert Camus suggested we should imagine Sisyphus, rolling his rock uphill, as content; in his Nobel-prize-winning novel *Fatelessness* (1975), the Hungarian Auschwitz-survivor Imre Kertész went so far as to evoke 'the happiness of the concentration camps'. Implausible though it may seem when viewed from the outside, when seen from the inside *all* experience is potentially valuable. The most emblematic of Holocaust victims understood this: to think of all the beauty around us, noted Anne Frank in a phos-phorous flash of defiance, is to be happy in that moment, however murderous the world beyond it may be. Beauty, in the immortal words of Stendhal, is *une promesse de bonheur*.

The problem is, the promise is so rarely fulfilled. The more educated we are, the more we are supposed to 'see through' life, to the hollowness of the human heart. We are taught how to see a text and raise its subtext; we are taught to call the bluff of beauty, to be suspicious of surfaces. We pride ourselves on not being 'taken in', on standing askance from the system. Pleasure, happiness, *joie de vivre* are suspect, simplistic, naïve, vestiges of childish credulity. Cynicism is the besetting sin of the intellectual.

What happened to optimism? What happened to my lust for life? Was it drummed out of me along with faith in humankind and belief in an omniscient narrator? The truth is, life's too fraught *not* to enjoy it; understand this, and we understand much of what drives us. Our capacity for intense sorrow is our capacity for intense happiness: tragicomedy is our defining genre. Without such extremes, our daily canvas becomes so much magnolia, bland background instead of bold colour. Those many moments – the meetings, the committees, the endless acronyms – when we feel we are merely skating across the surface of life, not taking risks and sounding the fathoms beneath us, are necessary but not transcendent. Things are fine, but the depth-charge is missing.

Literature – words, thoughts, the ideas of others – can provide this charge. To delight, and to teach us that delight matters in the first place, has been one of the traditional roles of writing ever since Horace. Across the various genres, joy is

– or should be – democratically distributed. Writing in 1817, Jane Austen suggests that 'the person, be it gentleman or lady, who has not pleasure in a good novel, must be intolerably stupid'. In 1925, Virginia Woolf states that the *essay* 'should give pleasure'. In 1942, Wallace Stevens notes that the *poem* 'must give us pleasure'. From the narrative satisfactions of a whodunnit to the cognitive complications of a lyric poem, from the storied brilliance of 'high' art to the studied brashness of low kitsch, precisely how such pleasure is to be defined remains a matter of endless debate. But pleasure there must be. We read for many reasons, just as we live for many reasons, but there is little point in doing so if it does not contribute, however indirectly, to our broader sense of life, liberty and the pursuit of happiness. Literary heroes, or antiheroes, can help us not just to be, but to be *happy*.

But how, exactly? Among the many original books of the French theorist Roland Barthes is his essay *The Pleasure of the Text* (1973), in which Barthes distinguishes between two kinds of literary enjoyment: *plaisir* and *jouissance*. If the former needs no translation, since pleasure speaks every language, the latter brooks no translation, conveying as it does both 'bliss' and 'orgasm'. In a very physical sense, literature can make us shiver with pleasure, on account of both its subject matter – it can, after all, be explicitly erotic, not to say pornographic – and its style. Reading can be a sensual experience: Vladimir Nabokov, one of the great stylists of both writing and reading, used to encourage his students to 'fondle the details'. In the words of the contemporary poet

David Constantine: 'the poem, like the clitoris, is there / for pleasure'.

Arresting though it undoubtedly is, Constantine's image distracts from what his syntax is saying, which is that poetry – as well, we may take it, as literature more generally – is there *for* something. The whole thrust of his statement, however, is that it is not there *for* anything; or rather that it is there for its own sake, for the sheer unadulterated pleasure of it. Art is good for nothing. It exists for no reason other than for itself. In this, art is like life: it must create its own purpose. *Un*like life, though, literature is a meaning-making machine, a controlled space in which the free play of the imagination mimics and models lived experience. Herein lies its value.

The paradox of Constantine's syntax, in other words, is that existing for *no* reason is tantamount to existing for *a* reason – because this reason is sheer gratuitous pleasure. If art is good for nothing, then it is good for everything. The argument is as old as aesthetics. The work of art, in the philosopher Immanuel Kant's seminal definition of 1790, constitutes 'purposiveness without purpose', which is another way of saying that it has no meaning outside of itself, that it must create its own meaning. This is why, many thinkers subsequent to Kant have argued, art can function as a moral tutor – not (just) because its conceits and conclusions are ethically edifying (the chastened hero, the happy ending), but because the very premise of art is that it enriches our imaginative engagement with the world. The pleasure of the text is also the pleasure of the context.

We all share this context, but we do not all see it the same way. Joy can be communal, but it is also individual. No two of us ever experience happiness in quite the same manner. The bliss is always keener in someone else's eyes. Art can help us see through these eyes, but in doing so it can also breed dissatisfaction. Why, my boys have asked me on more than one occasion after reading *The Lord of the Rings* or the latest Manga comic, is our own life not more adventurous? Why can we too not undertake a quest? But of course, we can and do: we just call it life. Reading helps us realise this, as we step in and out of our own adventures; writing helps us articulate this, projecting a sense of quest onto daily life. Literature offers a condensed version of existence. The shadow-puppetry of fiction brings us satisfaction, beyond its otherwise arbitrary organisation of letters on a page, precisely because it 'makes believe' – in meaning and conclusion, in the shape and structure that are so singularly lacking in our messy, intractable lives. In various senses of the term, we play on purpose.

The idea of play is crucial to any happy life. Article 31 of the UN Convention of the Rights of the Child enshrines it as a basic existential need, recognising 'the right of the child to rest and leisure, to engage in play and recreational activities appropriate to the age of the child and to participate freely in cultural life and the arts'. We all want to come out to play, and not just in childhood. Throughout our lives, we devote as much energy as possible to sport and leisure, sex and entertainment, as though these were the things that we really want to be doing, had we but world enough and time. But can we play our way into being better people? Such was the question that the German playwright and poet Friedrich Schiller posed in his letters *On the Aesthetic Education of Man* (1795).

Taking up Kant's ideas about 'purposiveness', Schiller used Kantian aesthetics – the question of how and why we appreciate art – to respond to contemporary politics, most obviously the recent French Revolution which had so shaken late-eighteenth-century Europe. Central to his response was the idea of the 'play-drive', which Schiller saw as the very essence of art. Autonomous, authentic art, 'purposeless' in the Kantian sense, encourages the development of this play-drive, which in turn powers the development of an 'aesthetic state'. This aesthetic state functions as a bridge between the 'physical state', in which we are dependent on nature, and the 'moral state', in which we master nature. Play thus leads to politics, aesthetic education to ethical freedom. *Homo ludens* is now master of himself.

The fact that this line of reasoning is profoundly Romantic, in both the lower- and upper-case senses of the term, helps us home in on our first lesson of literature for life. We cultivate the aesthetic state – we pursue the pleasure principle – in the full knowledge that it is *transient*, like life itself, and that this very transience is what constitutes its meaning. Everything ends: books teach us this if they teach us anything, that familiar sense of lurch and vertigo as we close the final page and look up again at the world. The happiest moments of my life have invariably been shadowed by a sense of this ephemerality. Falling in love, talking with friends, playing with children: this too will pass, I have always found myself thinking, this too *will have been*. Like a slave shadowing a Roman general at the moment of his greatest triumph, the future perfect shadows the present, whispering *memento mori* to us all.

The Romantic response to this passing is the much-apostrophised concept of 'beauty', as though beauty, if only it were sublime enough, could forestall the future. It is striking, in this context, how consistently such beauty derives from a sharpened sense of mortality. 'If I should die,' wrote John Keats to his fiancée Fanny Brawne in 1820, 'I have left no immortal work behind me [. . .] but I have lov'd the principle of beauty in all things.' That Keats *did* of course leave immortal work behind him provides the key to his Romantic aesthetics: art endures, and in so doing it transforms the impermanence of life into permanent beauty. 'A thing of beauty is a joy for ever'.

'The future perfect shadows the present, whispering memento mori *to us all.'*

Here, then, we seem to have an answer to the question of what art is for: ever. Yet when returned to the original context of his long poem *Endymion* (1818), it becomes clear that Keats's most celebrated single line derives its meaning not from unchanging timelessness, but from the way it sits in tension with the time*ful*ness of the human condition:

> A thing of beauty is a joy for ever:
> Its loveliness increases; it will never
> Pass into nothingness; but still will keep
> A bower quiet for us, and a sleep
> Full of sweet dreams, and health, and quiet breathing.
> Therefore, on every morrow, are we wreathing
> A flowery band to bind us to the earth,
> Spite of despondence, of the inhuman dearth
> Of noble natures, of the gloomy days,
> Of all the unhealthy and o'er-darkened ways
> Made for our searching: yes, in spite of all,
> Some shape of beauty moves away the pall
> From our dark spirits.

Keats's poem movingly expresses a simple truth, which is that beauty helps us survive our own meagre lives. We feel this intuitively, particularly as we get older: where the loveliness of created things 'increases', we mortals must 'pass into nothingness'. Our obsession with youth is an expression of this obvious fact. Eros accrues to early adulthood not just because these are, biologically speaking, the child-bearing years, but because they are also, psychologically speaking, the death-denying years. We like our celebrities young – which means, in the end, that we like them dead, since that is the only way that youth can endure.

24

Figure 1: A joy for ever?
Francesco Solimena, *Diana and Endymion* (c. 1710)

In the myth that Keats draws on, the goddesses are all enamoured of Endymion, the lovely shepherd boy. So they persuade Zeus to freeze him, to stop him from growing older. The 'shape of beauty' can only endure by becoming a *thing* of beauty, granted immortality at the price of eternal sleep. Art offers a crutch, or perhaps a compensation, for mortality – not just a spot of time, to use Wordsworth's great contemporary phrase, but a spot *out* of time, a way of assuaging our ageing egos. 'Seize me as I pass if you can,' writes Proust of one of his sudden surges of joy, 'and try to solve the riddle of happiness.'

Keats is also, naturally, commenting – how could he not be? – on his own poem. The beauty of music alleviates the ugliness of mortality; the pleasure palliates the pain. Poetry, with its hypnotic rhythms and heightened linguistic self-consciousness, arguably does this better than any genre, but all writing worthy of the name compels us to attend to its textures, to 'fondle the details'. I do it myself: the assonance of 'assuaging our ageing egos' assuages my own ageing ego, however pitiful its payoff. Reading and writing bring us pleasure, but they also teach us *how* to take pleasure. If 'carnal hermeneutics' has recently emerged as a mode of reading, a way of understanding words through bodily sensations, 'the art of slow reading' has been with us since Friedrich Nietzsche first articulated it in the late nineteenth century. Slowing us down – *sitting* us down, obliging us to attend more closely to the digressive anecdote or parenthetical aside – is not the least of literature's pleasures, and not the least of its lessons for life.

But it also, of course, speeds us up. The accelerating, escapist urgency of a 'good book' is clear to any child, let alone to an experienced reader. Well-chosen words are like rocket fuel: we curl up in our favourite armchair and let the story transport us, like a spaceship, to distant planets. That we don't yet know what is on those planets is part of the attraction; literature, unlike visual art, unfolds over time, its narrative pacing and cognitive 'suspense' an essential component of the conceptual striptease. In literature as in life, desire is what powers us forward. We want to know what happens next. The pleasure is in the yearning, not the destination.

However much is going on in our lives, however difficult things become, we can always take pleasure in slowing down or speeding up our mind's sigh. Whether bored on a slow day or bothered on a fast day, we can learn to regulate our internal speedometer by tuning our attention span to an external consciousness. Two versions of this tune emerge from two versions of literature.

'The pleasure is in the yearning, not the destination.'

On the one hand, there are certain kinds of stories – most obviously, detective fiction – that we read 'for the plot'. Tortured by the intolerable uncertainty of not knowing who committed the murder, we read on until we find out.

Highbrow critics tend to disdain this kind of writing as generic and middlebrow, but it is how most of us read – and *live* – most of the time. We want to know what happens next. Literature of this sort can be immensely compelling; not for nothing are Agatha Christie and John le Carré among the best-selling novelists in history. Hercule Poirot and George Smiley teach us, if we pay attention, how to appreciate characters and narratives, how to hunt for clues in the puzzle of our own lives. We, the reader, become the detective, inspectors of our own existence. There are worse ways to live.

Such plot-driven fiction is not designed to teach us anything. Yet it palpably does: how to escape ourselves. Escapism has a bad reputation – as *mere* escapism, as 'entertainment' – but art has always provided this. What is Aristotelian catharsis (Greek for cleansing, purification) if not a means of escaping or evacuating our emotions? What is wrong with being entertained? Sometimes I want nothing more than to forgo my own perspective, to forget my difficult colleagues and intractable problems. Sometimes I want to imagine that I am smarter than I really am, that I can crack the case and win the day. The thrill is in the chase, in the sheer disposable pleasure of finally learning how and why the butler – or in Woody Allen's joke about the dictionary, the zebra – did it. But the thrill is also in being someone else.

Set against this, there are certain kinds of literature that help us be ourselves. We enjoy such writing, whether lyric poetry or lyrical prose, principally for its style, for the way it is written. We are not so much drawn on by its content as drawn in by its form, by its arresting, exasperating, unsettling modes of expression, its felicity of formulation. Here the tension does not evaporate once we have got to the end of the story, since the story was never really the point in the first place, but rather the intricate articulation of states of consciousness. We can read such writing – Shakespearean monologues, Beckettian dialogues – again and again, insinuating our minds into every last nuance and cranny. Literature of this sort enriches both our appreciation of how we live, and our *perception* of how we live.

> *'I want precision, and I want playfulness.*
> *I want judgement, and I want joy.'*

These two kinds of writing represent not just two approaches to pleasure, but two approaches to meaning. Do we want to know who 'did' it, or do we want to alter our state of mind? Do we want to decode life, or to deepen it? Pushed to their limits, these positions articulate fundamental questions about the human condition, questions that are respectively scientific and aesthetic: is existence to be understood, or enjoyed?

Well I for one want both. I want to know more, and I want to live more. I want precision, and I want playfulness. I want judgement, and I want joy. It's worth thinking, though, about what happens when one half of the equation is emphasised over the other. What happens if we forget to enjoy life? What happens if we enjoy it too much? We can't exist just by going through the emotions; sometimes we need to get stuff done. But nor, equally, are we automata; sometimes we need to switch stuff off. Even the most workaholic of writers has to unplug from time to time. As someone who has always been terrible at enjoying holidays, I have long struggled with a nagging sense of guilt at the lost time, the opportunity cost, of doing nothing for three weeks. I'll never get this August back, I say to myself. But then I'll never get that August back either, the one where the evening sun beckons us to the beach as we freewheel lazily down the hill, ocean waves glistening beyond the handlebars. Unflinching focus has its own cost, the lost opportunities of obsessive-compulsive creativity. Art for art's sake can also be – *should* also be – life for life's sake.

The Aesthetes' mantra encapsulates, in many ways, the purposeless purpose of literature. Art for art's sake: when we think of the phrase, we emphasise, naturally enough, its repeated insistence on the currency of art. Yet the grammar of meaning, the syntax of 'sake', is equally important. The attempt to define meaning is perhaps the most striking characteristic of nineteenth-century Aestheticism. On the one hand, the Aesthetes sought to separate beauty and utility, as in the designer William Morris's epoch-making advice to 'have nothing in your house that you do not know to be useful or believe to be beautiful'. Yet on the other, they simultaneously attempted to fold them back together, into the recurring claim that beauty *is* utility. The two positions represent, in fact, opposite ends of the same claim, namely that art creates meaning – and that this, indeed, is its purpose. If the claim sounds almost transcendental, such was the context. As religious faith began receding in the wake of evolutionary theory (Darwin published *On the Origin of Species* in 1859), so artistic faith began taking its place. Now more than ever, art was required as a meaning-making machine.

The problem, however, is that what we consider beautiful – and what we consider 'artistic' – changes over time. The worst excesses of the Aesthetic style now seem horribly overwrought to us in the twenty-first century. 'A month or twain to live on honeycomb / Is pleasant; but one tires of scented time, / Cold sweet recurrence of accepted rhyme': Algernon Swinburne's lines 'Before Parting' (1875) both demonstrate and describe the problem. Pleasure is a relative concept, both because it can be so close to pain and because it is culturally contingent. We enjoy an activity or emotion because we have learned to enjoy it; there is no intrinsic reason why water polo is more or less enjoyable than wrestling. The same is true, clearly, of writing. There is nothing timelessly perfect about the Alexandrine or the post-modern novel – nor, indeed, about the Aesthetic prose style. 'We find ourselves marvelling at the words,' wrote Virginia Woolf of John Ruskin, 'as if all the fountains of the English language had been set playing in the sunlight for our pleasure'. But it is surely possible to have too many fountains.

'Perhaps we can learn to think of all the
ugliness *around us and be happy.'*

Such, at least, was the proposition of much of what we now think of as modernism. In one of the most consequential of all aesthetic reversals, beauty could be ugly; ugliness, writers and theorists began to discover in the late nineteenth century, could be beautiful. Literary histories often cite Charles Baudelaire's poem 'A Carcass' (1867) as the classic example of this reversal: 'that object we saw, dear soul, / in the sweetness of a summer morn' turns out to be 'a loathsome carrion [. . .] with legs raised like a lustful woman'. Baudelaire is not merely playing with the genre expectations of lyric poetry, luring us in before grossing us out – he is also encouraging us to attend to *all* the particularities of daily life, be they in the form of a romantic sunset or a rotting cadaver. 'Unflinching' is the adjective often ascribed to such art, to the attempt to show that scar tissue and carcasses also have a claim on our consciousness. If the trick of literature is to shock us into paying attention, then 'beauty' becomes a moving target, one constantly waiting, like the meaning of life itself, to be redefined in the light of lived experience. Perhaps we can learn to think of all the *ugliness* around us and be happy.

We can only do so, though, because in the end art does not matter – or rather, because it matters a great deal precisely by not mattering at all. Art, like sport, is perfectly gratuitous, and therein lies its great lesson for life. For what is living, too, if not a kind of purposiveness without purpose? Without belief in some transcendental deity, what exterior meaning is there? Nietzsche, the great theorist of this question, saw in art the balm for our Godforsaken modernity. Once God had been declared dead, the conscious cultivation of superficiality – purposiveness without purpose – was the surest way to protect ourselves from the void. If secular modernity has condemned us to creating our own meaning, then art, and in particular literature, with its ability to reflect on its own premises, can help us to create this meaning. Art for art's sake becomes life for life's sake: taking pleasure becomes its own purpose. The pleasure principle becomes, *faute de mieux*, the meaning principle. The beach beckons once again.

The pleasure principle, as Freud famously defined it, consists in the immediate gratification of desire. It is the driving force of what he called the Id, the instinctive urge to self-interest that defines all living things, and specifically the infantile stage of human development. As we grow older, we learn – or we *should* learn – to repress our instincts through the intervention of the Super-ego. By this means a balanced ego emerges, in the healthy adult, as the basis for mature social interaction. Scaled up from the individual specimen to the collective species, the model comes to define, as Freud sees it, society as a whole. In *Civilisation and its Discontents* (1930) he suggests that the whole process of 'civilising' human relations amounts to the repression of base instinct. Self-interest must be tempered by disinterest.

However antiquated they may now seem, Freud's terms provide a useful rough-and-ready basis for thinking about what it means to have desires and to seek pleasures. We oscillate between interest in ourselves and interest in others – indeed, we learn to develop beyond ourselves *by* showing an interest in others. Reading is one of the most powerful ways in which we can do so, both as unformed children and as informed adults. Yet the moral lessons of literature would be unpalatable were they not sweetened with pleasure, whether through the perfectly balanced sentence or the perfectly plotted story. In the classical terms of Horace, we need both the *dulce* and the *utile*: seduced by sweetness, we become useful to ourselves and to the world outside us. We progress, in other words, from the aesthetics of beauty to its ethics.

Such is the force of our first commandment: think of all the beauty around you and be happy. But it is also the force of literature, which is almost uniquely placed both to embody and to encourage the cultivation of joy as the cultivation of meaning. 'Show, don't tell', creative writing classes are forever instructing us. Yet writing can show *and* tell. In showing us the example of its verbal felicity, it tells us how to live better, fuller lives. 'You must change your life', runs the celebrated closing imperative of Rainer Maria Rilke's poem 'Archaic Torso of Apollo' (1908): while it is the sculpture that shows us this, it is the sonnet that *tells* us this. Only words can both convey and conceptualise. Only words can bring us joy while articulating the parameters – the physical limits, the metaphysical possibilities – of such joy. To tell someone to *be* happy is facile; there is no simple switch, alas, that can be flicked on and off. To show them *how* to be happy, though – this is the stuff that dreams, and stories, are made on.

II

Find your narrative arc

Lesson two: Be the hero of your own life

'Whether i shall turn out to be the hero of my own life, or whether that station will be held by anybody else, these pages must show.' The opening lines of *David Copperfield* map out, with genre-defining clarity, one of the fundamental questions of fiction. Who is the protagonist?

One possible answer would be that we all are. I am, you are, he or she is. I sit here writing this; you are now reading it; he or she, with any luck, might soon discover it. The changing pronouns pace out our changing perspectives: we see things differently depending on where we are sitting. For better or worse, we are all fated to play the central role in our own existence. There is no doubt, though, that some of us are more forcefully, more successfully, more *fully* ourselves than others. Some of us are heroes as well as protagonists. The shifting relationship between the two terms comes down to the shifting relationship between our views of ourselves as more or less achieved, more or less fulfilled human beings.

The hero is he who is immovably centred, wrote the great American hero Ralph Waldo Emerson; whether we shall turn out to be the centre of our own existence is a key question not only of literature, but also of life. How are we to make the most of our brief time on earth?

The classic biographical structure from birth to death provides a ready-made framework for how to see our lives. Whether we can find our own version of it, however, depends on whether we can find our own narrative arc. It's easy enough to look back – born in Winchester, bred in school, broadened through travel, I can construct a narrative of my own life with little effort. But the real question is how to look forward. Where am I going? How will I get there? And am I even at the centre of my own existence? The arc of the moral universe may bend towards justice, in the immortal words of Martin Luther King, but mere mortals cannot wait that long. The question for our own finite lives, trivial though they may ultimately be, is whether the arc bends towards meaning.

In the Dickensian version, the extent to which we are our own main character depends on the telling. Narcissism begets narrative. Dickens himself seems to have intuited as much, reversing his initials CD into those of his protagonist DC. We are, in effect, the stories we tell about – and to – ourselves. The stiff, Germanic syntax of Dickens's opening sentence foregrounds the question of self-determination right from the start. By inverting the standard order of the clauses, he lends dramatic force to mundane statement: 'These pages must show [. . .] whether I shall turn out to be the hero.' If there is a kind of false narrative modesty at work here (Copperfield *knows* how the story turns out before relating it, so he is only feigning ignorance), such is the conceit of literature: the author invites us, with his very first word 'whether', to suspend not so much disbelief as judgement. It is in the nature of lived experience that our judgement is unavoidably inflected by the prejudices and preconceptions that we bring to the book. Fiction – sentence, syntax and sensibility – furnishes an existential prism through which to see not only Copperfield's development, but also that of ourselves and our friends. Onto the arc of others we project our own. How can we not?

Finding this arc is one of the core imperatives of creative writing courses, whether for the page or for the screen. If there is a certain cheesiness to the challenge – finding your arc is a close cousin to 'finding yourself' – it is because the experience is universal. Aspiring writers are forever being told that their characters must undergo a 'journey', understood as the development of ethical and interpersonal insights withheld at the start of a given story but vouchsafed by the end. Events must give us pause, and then propel us into otherwise unattainable states of being. Chased by enemies, chastened by experience, protagonists become heroes by virtue of their newfound psychological and emotional maturity. The technique is so ubiquitous in contemporary culture that we barely recognise it for what it is – namely precisely that, a technique, from the Greek *tekhnē*, meaning an 'art, skill, or craft'. The art, skill or craft in question is that of the novel, invented in early modernity but reaching full maturity only with the advent of industrialisation in the nineteenth century: a recognisably modern genre for a recognisably modern experience.

The novel in its classical form provides the blueprint not just for contemporary forms of leisure, such as the boxset series or the character-driven film, but for contemporary forms of life. So much of our self-image, and of our attempts to live out and up to that self-image, is fashioned as a kind of *Bildungsroman*, where the possibility of our continuing progress is the precondition for *amour-propre*. Self-improvement is big business: to stay as we are is to stagnate as we are, left behind by the self-optimisers of 'personal development'. We all want to keep evolving in our careers and our private lives, in our bodies and our cultural lives, not just because we fear stasis but because our very sense of self-worth is predicated on constant evolution. All those gym classes and language lessons, all those cookery courses and yoga retreats: we want nothing so much as to keep moving. Nature abhors inaction.

The *Bildungsroman* raises this movement into its own sense of purpose. The term – literally, 'novel of education' – was coined by the philologist Karl Morgenstern in 1819, codifying the idea of *Bildung* that had emerged out of Romanticism as one of the central tenets of Germanic culture. *Bildung* implies a mixture of intellectual, emotional and ethical education: we are *gebildet* when we are mature, morally speaking. The process maps most directly onto the period of adolescence, when we are still immature but hungry to be older. (At what point do we stop wanting to be older?) I remember first encountering the concept as a teenager yearning to be taken seriously as an adult. The Germanic term dignified the messiness of immaturity, giving it an air of sophistication wholly unmerited by my own banal adolescence. But it captured the education to which I aspired.

Romanticism showed that art could provide one of the principal vehicles for such education. Yet it was only with the arrival of Realism, in the middle of the nineteenth century, that *Bildung* became a defining element of a literary genre – and by extension, of the way that we conceive our lives more generally. Self-improvement, by the mid-1800s, had become a Realistic prospect. The idea of the narrative arc, as we understand it now and apply it to our sense of our careers' and lives' unfolding towards ever greater meaning, is a direct descendant of this nineteenth-century notion of *Bildung*. The tension of the arc is the drive to development: we all have great expectations of our own lives, at least until experience teaches us otherwise. Casting ourselves as the protagonists of our autobiographies, we struggle towards what Aristotle called *anagnorisis*, the moment of true insight into our characters and capabilities.

'We all have great expectations of our own lives, at least until experience teaches us otherwise.'

The trick of Realist fiction is to project this struggle – and our *understanding* of this struggle – onto created consciousness. Such artificiality enhances, rather than impedes, experience. We enjoy reading novels (or watching television series) because we identify, at least to a certain extent, with the perspective of the protagonists. For the duration of the book, their jeopardy becomes our jeopardy, even if in carefully contained, carefully quarantined form. We may be bored like Emma Bovary, misguided like Dorothea Brooke or ostracised like Anna Karenina, but we can both experience these emotions and step back from them. The distance afforded by fiction is as important as its ability to encourage identification.

This is why the secret weapon of Realism, its true *tekhnē*, is the manipulation of narrative perspective. The Realist novel unfolds, in general, through what is known as free indirect discourse. The story is told from the point of view of a protagonist in such a way that we see things through their eyes and their thoughts – but are not, crucially, beholden to them. Third-person perspectives, in particular, leave room for the reader to pursue alternative interpretations (the more panoramic of Realist novels with their wide range of characters, such as *Middlemarch* or *War and Peace*, are particularly good at this). We can sympathise with a character's predicament while being gently led, through the offices of the narrator, to the realisation – as yet unclear to the character herself – that she may be wrong about it. Despite the clichés, Realism is not just about the socio-economic consequences of industrialisation – it is also about consciousness.

For us as readers, naturally enough, this means *self*-consciousness. The free indirect discourse is as much that of the reader as of the narrator. As we turn the pages, as we project ourselves onto the lives of the characters, we are inevitably also thinking about our own concerns. The major milestones of my life – childhood, college, children – are the major milestones of your life, but the details are different. And it is the details that make me *me* and you *you*, the half-remembered, misremembered moments that exist only in our minds, the split lip and wounded pride of tenacious interiority. I did not fall off my bike at exactly the same time or place that you did; but nor, of course, did I fall off my bike in exactly the way that I think I did. I did not have the same schoolfriends that you did; but nor did I have exactly the schoolfriends that I remember, distorted as their memory has become through time and circumstance. We are all unreliable narrators, not least because we experience so much of our lives vicariously. There is only so much that we can see, hear or feel in person.

'We are all unreliable narrators.'

The great advantage of Realist fiction is that it allows us, like a virtual reality machine, to adopt this vicarious perspective. Seeing things through the eyes of others is more than mere displacement activity, since it informs in turn our perception of our own lives. If I commit to reading a book, then that book becomes, however modestly, a part of my unfolding story, a part of my flailing, failing attempts to become a more intelligent, more capacious person. Finding my narrative arc, in this regard, means exploring alternatives; owning my life means experiencing that of others. What Flaubert terms 'sentimental education' – the very definition of the *Bildungs-roman* – is as much a fictional as a factual construct.

Which of us, after all, does not require educating in our sentiments? If imaginative literature is a surpassingly good tutor, it is not just because it teaches us to recognise ideas or emotions such as love, humility or forgiveness, but because it enlarges our range of ideas and emotions in the first place. The rise of the novel in the eighteenth century illustrates this neatly, particularly through the emergence of its epistolary form. The three major examples of the genre in the three major traditions of English, French and German literature – Samuel Richardson's *Clarissa* (1748), Rousseau's *Julie; or, the New Heloise* (1761) and Goethe's *The Sufferings of Young Werther* (1774) – effectively created a new mode of reading, one that encouraged empathy and identification with fictional heroes and heroines. That they also encouraged *over*-identification is the stuff of literary legend. 'I verily believe I have shed a pint of tears', declared Richardson's friend Lady Dorothy Bradshaigh on reading *Clarissa*; 'I loved with Werther, suffered with Werther, died with Werther', declared the German playwright J.M.R. Lenz. Individual taste, and the very notion of taste, created a new cult of 'sensibility'.

Significantly, however, it was the form of the novels as much as their content that elicited these tears, by inviting readers to see events from the unmediated perspective of the protagonists. The epistolary novel 'provided training not only in sympathy but also in empathy', in the words of one recent historian of the Enlightenment, Ritchie Robertson. Allowing readers to follow events in real time, the use of letters seemed to dissolve the barrier between fact and fiction, life and literature, culminating in the notorious – although probably apocryphal – copycat suicides of Werther. Young men took to wearing Werther's famous yellow waistcoat in the way that teenagers now wear their favourite band's T-shirt, as a signal of sensitivity and identity. Storm and stress were all the rage.

In this post-Enlightenment period, literature came to be seen as a vehicle of both moral and sentimental education, as Adam Smith captured in his *Theory of Moral Sentiments* (1759) when praising 'poets and romance writers' as 'much better instructors' than philosophers and thinkers. By projecting themselves onto a protagonist, readers could become the protagonist; by dressing or thinking like Werther, they could become Werther. Two and a half centuries later, we do this all the time, identifying with celebrities or immersing ourselves in virtual worlds, forever shoring up our fragile sense of self. Without pretence, without pretension, we cannot develop: when I first began writing I wanted to publish under the name 'B.W. Hutchinson', as though the initials would somehow confer on me the status of modernist poets like T.S. Eliot or W.B. Yeats. Our own identity, our own arc, is a composite of others, a mishmash of mimetic desire. Reading, with what Smith calls its 'moderated sensibility to the misfortunes of others', is a prime generator of such desire.

The sentimental education of nineteenth-century literature rehearsed the sentimentality of the eighteenth century, but in more distanced, mediated form. Romanticism gave way to Realism. As the first-person epistolary perspective gave way to third-person indirect discourse, so readers developed a more nuanced relationship to literary protagonists. Stories of Victorians crying over Dickens, for instance, recall the affective provocations of the epistolary novel a hundred years earlier; but they also led to a backlash, with one anonymous author thundering in 1867 that Britain was 'flooded with a perfect inundation of sentimentality far above anything known or seen before'. Oscar Wilde's *bon mot*, that one would have to have a heart of stone not to laugh at the death of Little Nell, encapsulates the shift in sensibility. Sentimentality gave way to irony.

It hardly needs adding that this shift in perspective informs how we see our own lives. We tell ourselves stories in order to live, in the much cited words of Joan Didion, but we also live in order to tell ourselves stories. Life picks up where literature finishes, the happy ever after taken seriously. The major existential decisions, whether choosing a career, getting married or having children, are so many stories that we choose to start, predications of a happy, hopeful future. To get these decisions right, though, we have to realise that they could be different, that there is no single storey to the building of our lives. We could all be equally fulfilled in another job, another relationship, another life; to admit this is not to undermine the one that we have, but to acknowledge the importance of commitment – of *conscious* commitment – as a prerequisite of purpose. I remember realising that I wanted to marry Marie; I remember realising that I wanted to live across more than one country; I remember realising that I wanted to dedicate my life to words and ideas. Just as we have to *want* to be happy, so we have to want to live meaningfully.

'Finding your narrative arc often means losing it first.'

Sometimes, though, we need to step outside ourselves to see this. Sometimes we need to move from the first person to the third person, from the white-hot pangs of Romantic poetry to the cooler pleasures of Realist prose. Just as distance, in Realist fiction, is as important as identification, so self-distance, in realistic life, is as important as self-identification. Escapism is as necessary as empathy to the good life: who doesn't get tired of being themselves? If other people's lives, like other people's parents, often seem more alluring, it is because we are not subject to their strictures and limitations. Finding your narrative arc often means losing it first.

By the time of modernism in the early twentieth century, self-alienation of this sort had become an article of faith. 'In

order to possess what you do not possess,' in the words of
T.S. Eliot, 'you must go by the way of dispossession.' Franz
Kafka, perhaps the most truly representative of all twentieth-
century writers, shows us this better than anyone. With just a
small shift into underexplained anonymity, Kafka's protagonists mirror back our world to us with nauseous, nightmarish
clarity. The Realist writers whom he revered – Flaubert,
Dickens – are never far away, but now they are turned inside
out. All detail of circumstance and causation is deliberately
suppressed, the better to convey the impenetrability of imper-
sonal, incomprehensible bureaucracies. Kafka's novels, in this
regard, are anti-*Bildungsromane*: things get regressively worse,
rather than progressively better. Like Josef K. in *The Trial*,
we don't know why we have been accused – we don't know
why we are alive – so we can only flail around vainly for elusive handholds. In the chaos of modernity, Kafka teaches us,
we can*not* find our narrative arc, for to do so would imply a
stable structure of meaning in the first place. Without God
the Father, we are disinherited.

Yet Kafka also teaches us – and such is the great lesson of
modern art – that this insight itself is worth having. Once
Darwin and Nietzsche had pronounced the death of God, it
became clear not only that we had to find our own meaning,
but that the very *search* for meaning would henceforth structure our lives. It is not the finding of the narrative arc that
matters, so much as the seeking. What is the novel if not a
machine for structuring this search? What is literature if not
a means of articulating alternative ways of thinking, of living?

To find our narrative arc, we must believe that we have one in the first place.

Commandment number two amounts, then, to a simple imperative: live as though you were following a trajectory. The truth is, of course, we are all making it up as we go along – but who can live that way? Plans, projects and plotlines are indispensable to our sense of ourselves as future-oriented animals, however aft they gang agley. Both mice and men must keep laying schemes; both must live as though they have control over their destinies, even if in reality so very often they do not. The philosophy of *as if*, to cite the title of an influential book of 1911 by the German thinker Hans Vaihinger, is what helps us look beyond today to tomorrow and the day after. We must live *as if* we knew where we were heading. The future, as we understand it, is a necessary fiction.

It is in the nature of such fiction that it sometimes leads us astray. Literature muddles us as much as it models us. *Don Quixote*, the very earliest European novel, tells the salutary tale of a man who has read too much, or at least drawn the wrong lessons from his overheated reading. Which of us doesn't occasionally feel this way? All the words in the world can't compensate for lived experience if they shut us *off* from lived experience, from the rattle and scrape of raw reality. Quixote's inability to distinguish between life and literature as he takes windmills for giants, and mistakes basins for helmets, is what drives the comedy. But the joke is on us, since this blurring of boundaries becomes the basis for the Western novel. Don Quixote the character loses himself in imagined battles so

Figure 2: The man who read too much: Honoré Daumier,
Don Quixote and the Windmills, c. 1850

that Cervantes the author can find his way out of real battles (he famously lost an arm fighting at Lepanto in 1571). The mock-heroic protagonist fashions the heroic author just as much as the other way around.

How, then, do we turn ourselves from protagonists into heroes? The answer, literature helps us to see, is not just to find our narrative arc, but to *create* it. It is not enough passively to observe the stories of others; we must actively extrapolate to our own lives. It is not enough merely to read; we must also write – not necessarily in the literal sense of putting pen to paper, but in the broader sense of sketching out our own plotlines. For the key difference between literature and life is that the former lies complete before us – the poem or novel is always finished *before* we read it – whereas the latter we experience in real time, *in medias res*. We have agency; we have free will; but we do not yet have the whole story.

This is why I have always objected to the Aristotelian idea of *hamartia*, the fatal flaw that predetermines a protagonist's downfall. It is too neat and tidy, too unerringly prefabricated. The doomed hero of ancient tragedy may possess a certain dark glamour – Oedipus fated to kill his father, Icarus destined to soar too high – but his narrative arc is overdetermined, at least to our modern mentality. What we want in our twenty-first-century lives, surely, is to be *self*-determined, to assert our own 'main character energy'. While Aristotle claims that character in a play reveals moral purpose, in real life moral purpose reveals character, or at least the attempt to cultivate it.

In practice, this means that our sense of our evolving lives advances like a hermeneutic circle, a term that philosophers use to refer to the way we understand texts as a constant negotiation between part and whole. In life, too, we are forever making readjustments between the part that we do know and the whole that we do not; looking back, we don't always realise just how much the part inflects the whole. In making adjustments to our present, perhaps by changing job, moving house, or starting a new relationship, we are also defining our future. Twenty years have passed, and here I still am in the same job, the same house, the same relationship. Happiness and purpose are a wager on the long term, on the length of the arc as it bends towards meaning. By definition – or rather, by *lack* of finition, the absence of an ending – the outcome of the wager is uncertain, unlike in Greek tragedy; but we have to make it. To paraphrase Pascal, we bet on the existence of plot, on the unfolding of our lives towards resolution. Call no man happy, in the words of Herodotus's Croesus, until just before he dies, because it is only then that he will be able to survey the totality of his life.

'To paraphrase Pascal, we bet on the existence of plot.'

Creating the narrative arc of our lives, in other words, means something different to finding it in literature, since we don't yet know the ending. We are making it up as we go along: fiction helps us reclaim the insult as a compliment. Making things up is the way we *should* be living, situating ourselves on a continuum of purpose between what is and what might be, between dependence and independence. It means creating our own stories, our own text and context; it means asserting, where necessary, our distance from those around us, be they family, friends or mere contemporaries. It means, above all, learning how to transcend our circumstances. We may then become, through the imagination, not simply creatures of chance contingent upon the hazard of our birth, but citizens of other times and places, too. 'Live in your century,' advises Schiller, 'but do not be its creature.'

It is *your* arc that you seek, not someone else's. Literature, by showing us the imagined example of others, teaches us this basic truth. 'To become morally independent of one's formative society', writes the critic William Empson magnificently, 'is the grandest theme of all literature, because it is the only means of moral progress, the establishment of some higher ethical concept.' Education leads to emancipation; *Bildung* leads to autonomy. The final aim of the *Bildungsroman* is not to become like others, but to become *un*like others: to become yourself.

III

Make space for others

Lesson three: It's not about you

IMAGINE HAVING A MACHINE that you could climb into every time you wanted to become someone else. Imagine the sights it could show you, the stories it could tell you, the ideas it could give you. Imagine, moreover, that this machine was endowed with its own consciousness – no Turing test required – and could comment back to you on what you were hearing, in real time, as events unrolled before you. Imagine, now, not just the sights it could show you, but the feelings it could give you – the feeling, above all, of inhabiting someone else's point of view, of having access to their innermost thoughts and reactions. Imagine, in short, someone else's imagination.

Life, like literature, is not just about finding your own arc. It is also about exploring someone else's, about learning to see the world through other eyes – and about learning to see that there *are* other eyes in the first place. The basis of all religion, and of all morality, is that not everything is about you; it is one of the hardest lessons we learn in childhood, if indeed we ever do. It is not just our fathers and mothers whom we should honour – they function, in any case, as a retrospective extension of the self – but everyone else, too: our sisters and our brothers, our friends and our acquaintances. The commandment is to cognisance of others.

Such cognisance is as much a question of aesthetics as of ethics. It is all very well being told to respect other people and to empathise with their situation, but how do we know what it feels like to be in their skin if we have not also been in their heads? Like everyone else, I'm limited to the life that I have had – in my case, white, middle class, male, the epitome of Western privilege. Short of gender reassignment, I can't change these basic facts of my inheritance, but I can be curious about the perspective of others. I can imagine someone else's imagination.

A recent experience with my running group brought home to me the limits of my own imagination. Jogging across the Kent downs on a beautiful May evening, we turned a corner at the edge of a field and were brought to a sudden halt. Our carefree chatter stopped immediately: a younger man was bent over an older man, who was prone on the ground and had evidently just collapsed. The abandoned bicycles and bucolic setting belied a desperate scene. The man had stopped breathing. Try as we might to resuscitate him – pump-starting his chest, jump-starting him with a defibrillator – he did not respond. As the spring sunlight fell softly across the country lane, a man lay dying.

That such an encounter lingers in the memory is hardly surprising. It's almost biblical in its simplicity: the dying father, the disconsolate youth. What has stayed with me from this sad story, though, is not so much the arbitrary nature of life and death – with its concomitant cliché *carpe diem*, since you never know what is around the corner of the next field – as the inaccessibility of personal experience. What has stayed with me is not so much the older man's passing – he was gone, that much was evident – as the younger man's grief, the distress of the poor son who watched his father collapse and die in front of him. We did our best to console him, but he was on a different timeline, experiencing the world in a different way to us. He was not just inconsolable but incommunicable, a mute animal reduced to moaning and shaking. What has stayed with me is the privacy of pain.

How can we feel his pain, or that of anyone else? *I can only imagine* how he is feeling, runs the saying. But can I? Even recounting this story runs the risk of appropriating it, prettifying it, turning it into just another edifying anecdote – or worse still, an opportunity for personal 'growth'. Surely it is better to imagine it not from my perspective, but from that of the grieving son; to foreground his version, not mine. The question, though, is how to access his version. Pious assertions of brotherly love only get us so far. Rather than loving thy neighbour, why not *be* thy neighbour, at least for the duration of a novel or narrative, a poem or play. Why not be someone else? Here, in essence, is the difference between self-help and art. Art is not about indulging the self; it is about encountering the other. Art shows us the *limits* of the self by exposing us to the gaze, however mute and inconsolable, of the grieving other.

From Sophocles to C.S. Lewis, from Barthes to Didion, literature does not lack for accounts of grief. German has a term for it, as only German can: *Trauerarbeit*, the work of mourning that responds, and in some sense gives meaning, to the sense of irreparable loss. Private work enables public feeling: catharsis for the author produces compassion in the reader. We come around the corner of our own perspective and realise, with a jolt, that others have more pressing concerns than we do. Imagined experience can evoke this sensation as effectively as real experience. When a friend told me that a character in the novel she was writing had cancer, I remember involuntarily responding, 'I'm very sorry to hear that.' It was a joke, of course, but only partially. Literature can catch us cold just like life.

It would be a mistake, however, to think that the imagination solves all our problems. Empathy cannot be asserted through a simple act of will. For one thing, we can never fully adopt someone else's perspective, since we can never fully stop being ourselves. The greatest artists are those who come closest to this state of supreme sensitivity, but it is a dangerous, mortally exposed condition. As George Eliot movingly writes in *Middlemarch* (1871–2), 'If we had a keen vision and feeling of all ordinary human life, it would be like hearing the grass grow and the squirrel's heart beat, and we should die of that roar which lies on the other side of silence.' Even at our most selfless, we retain our defensive deafness, our accumulated baggage of prejudice and experience. Even when looking at the world from someone else's perspective, we are always also looking from our own. Unlike the Faustian figure of Peter Schlemihl – the creation of the Romantic poet Adalbert von Chamisso, who wrote in German to escape his native French Revolution – we cannot sell our shadow to the devil.

> *'Even at our most selfless, we retain our*
> *defensive deafness.'*

Literature, however, does not ask us to do this. If anything, it makes a conceptual virtue out of cognitive necessity. It enables us to see someone else's outline while retaining, as we must, our own. If we cannot help but cast a shadow even when looking through someone else's eyes, why not amplify this split sensibility? Why not see the world in stereo? Writing, even about yourself, is never just about yourself, since there is always an implied reader. Reading, even about someone else, is never just about someone else, since you are always the implied needer. In the memorably simple statement of the poet Nicolas Born, a key figure of the West German intelligentsia of the 1970s whose politics were based on the ethics of shared experience: 'I am not enough by myself / The number of my chairs proves it'.

Figure 3: Escaping your own shadow:
Adelbert von Chamisso, *Peter Schlemihl* (1814)

Literature incorporates this insight into its very structures. To the basic contract between author and reader can be added the split sensibilities of narrator and protagonist(s), an effect which is compounded once these protagonists themselves start narrating their own stories. As it unfolds, in other words, a text may rapidly come to contain five or six overlayered perspectives. Some writers – postmodernists such as Italo Calvino, prose stylists such as W.G. Sebald – are masters of this multiple voice, able to convey through the frameworks of their narrative the layers of history underlying contemporary experience. The vertigo that this produces is part of the point, unsettling our settled view of things. We are forced to reflect on how consciousness is in effect a palimpsest of past and present.

Writing of this sort can help us see the world through the eyes not just of *an*other, but of *others*. Sebald, borrowing a term from the Austrian author Thomas Bernhard, called this technique 'periscopic', meaning that through adopting multiple narrative perspectives we can peep out from under the surface of our own element and see the air above us. That this is both an ethical and an aesthetic undertaking is immediately obvious. Kant famously wrote that 'two things fill the mind with ever new and increasing admiration and awe [. . .]: the starry heavens above me and the moral law within me'. But what about the moral law *without* me? By pointing above and beyond ourselves, the periscope of literature enables us to see the starry heavens as they appear to others.

What a periscope also does, of course, is foreshorten

distances, making things appear closer than they really are. Defined in such terms, literature offers a microcosm of the constant negotiation between proximity and distance that characterises all human interaction. Reading can help collapse distances between us and others, but by the same token it can also help *create* distances between us and our own presuppositions. Maintaining our distance, not so much from each other as from *ourselves*, is one of the fundamental challenges of the human condition, haunted as it is by the banality of ego. How can we learn – how can we continue to learn – to see ourselves from *outside*? How can we keep our distance from ourselves?

Cultivating this distance is the very basis of the humanities. Everything that we study in the arts, in history and philosophy, in languages and literatures, is about learning what the world looks like and sounds like from somewhere else. There's an old joke about someone who stops to ask for directions and promptly receives the response: I wouldn't start from here. Studying the culture of the past and present is precisely a way of *not* starting from here, of overcoming our own inbuilt bias to self-obsession. Each of us aspires to be the hero of our own story – but how does our story look to others? We all hate seeing ourselves on film, or hearing ourselves on radio, because it reminds us that the world views us very differently to how we view ourselves. To learn what it means to be human is to learn not just what it means to be oneself, and not just what it means to be another person – but what it means to see oneself *as* another person.

We rarely reflect, though, on how this process works. What is the psychology of reading? If stage one is to adopt some-one else's perspective, it is almost immediately followed, if we are being honest, by stage two, which is to compare it to our own. How often do we read a novel, an essay or a biography and wonder how we match up? How often do we project our-selves as the secret hero? Nothing dies harder than the desire to think well of oneself, in the words of T.S. Eliot; narcissism is native, and it is evergreen. With luck and self-discipline, we can hope to attain stage three, an ability to take a genuine (dis)interest in others. Our timber is so crooked, though, that it is hardly a natural state.

> *'Nothing dies harder than the desire to think well of oneself.'*
>
> T.S. ELIOT

Even if reading *can* help mitigate our native narcissism, in any case, it is far from obvious that writing has the same effect. Yeats claimed that 'out of the quarrel with others we make rhetoric; out of the quarrel with ourselves we make poetry', and a degree of self-absorption may be necessary to be con-sistently creative, at least in a genre as intimate as lyric verse. For such poetry to speak to others, though, it must be open to others; it must listen, as well as talk. All literature worthy of the name, even the most self-involved of odes or elegies, is not just about the author – otherwise it would only be of interest to the author. Even now, as I type these words, I am trying to articulate not just my own pursuit of purpose, but that of the mythical beast, hunted to near extinction, known as the 'common reader', the educated non-specialist. We have to find ways of speaking to each other as well as to ourselves.

These essays are caught in the same conundrum. Like all writers, I can only begin from my own perspective. Moral intransigence – the stubborn belief that I have something to say – is part of the project. How else can I put pen to paper? In this regard, writing is like a conjuring act, a rope trick with language: we climb up the words as we type them, convincing ourselves of their tautness and tension for fear that they will go slack and let us fall. But the reader has to believe in the rope, too, else it collapses under the weight of its own con-tradictions. In literature as in life, self-confidence must also mean confidence in our place in the world.

> *'Writing is like a conjuring act, a rope trick with language.'*

If reading and writing both make space for others, then, they do so in very different ways. Where the former is necessarily a dialogue, the latter can amount, at times, to a monologue, albeit a monologue with an implicit audience (does a monologue that falls in a forest still make a sound?).

The Russian poet Osip Mandelstam compared poetry to a 'message in a bottle', cast out from the island of the self in the hope – but not the certainty – that it would find a recipient. The point of the image is not that the message does or does not find its reader, but that the very act of casting it out constitutes an attempt at communication. In the words of the American-Palestinian critic Edward Said, art is 'all about a voyage to the "other"' – a view, he added, that is in the minority today.

Said's exemplar for this view is Goethe's late interest in Islam, as expressed through the German poet's reworkings of the Persian poet Hafiz in the *West-Eastern Divan* (1819). The tradition of adopting a 'Persian' perspective from the European point of view had been established a century earlier by the French writer Montesquieu in his *Persian Letters* (1721). This series of fictional missives is written as if by two supposed noblemen, Usbek and Rica, as they travel around France. Like all good French exchange students, Usbek and Rica end up, inevitably, in Paris. Montesquieu describes the city as 'a shared homeland for all foreigners' – which includes, in this case, fictional foreigners.

By adopting the Persian perspective, Montesquieu defamiliarises the familiarity of Europe. His imagined spectacles are like X-ray glasses, seeing through the all too familiar surface of Paris in the dog days of Louis XIV's reign to the essential strangeness at the heart of all human society. Usbek and Rica look askance at religious, political, cultural and sexual customs that a Frenchman of the day would never question, since it would never occur to the Frenchman that things could be any other way. Perpetually astonished by everything they encounter, the Persian travellers spend their life 'examining' the European society that the Europeans themselves take for granted. Montesquieu creates a kind of anthropology of the everyday.

Of course, the misadventures of Uzbek and Rica are also meant as a satire of contemporary *moeurs*, and Montesquieu has much fun skewering the vanities of the French court (many members of which, for instance, were all too eager to acquire aristocratic titles by donating to the royal finances). But there is also a serious psychological point here. As Rica notes in one letter, 'we only ever judge things through secretly bringing them back to us'; if triangles had a God, he suggests by way of illustration, He would have three sides. To this extent, we are all triangular: we all imagine life as a continuation of our own concerns. By stepping outside our own three sides – if only through the imagined perspective of a Persian Parisian – we can hope to conceive other shapes and forms, to gain some measure of mastery over our otherwise unquestioned geometries of thinking and living.

My brief history of the 'Persian perspective' illustrates the essential point of our third commandment: we must make space for others. From Montesquieu to Goethe to Said, from French to German to English, writers of the eighteenth, nineteenth and twentieth centuries gain purchase on one position by imagining – or by critiquing – another. With all its 'orientalist' pitfalls, the East–West opposition provides a striking example of the ways in which literature can help us explore alternative perspectives to our own. It is incumbent on those of us raised principally in one tradition to try to imagine and explore another.

The moral force of such imaginative effort disarms in advance Samuel Huntingdon's 'clash of civilisations', privileging encounter over antagonism. The onus to make space for others plays itself out at the collective as well as the individual level. To read, for example, Ibn Khaldun's great work of history, the *Muqaddimah* (1377), is to learn how medieval Europe looked from an Arabic perspective. To read *I, Rigoberta Menchú* (1983) is to learn what it means to be an indigenous Central American woman (albeit articulated, ironically, through the colonial language of Spanish). Reading does not just teach you that it's not about you; it also teaches us that it's not about us.

Too much reading, conversely, has the opposite effect. The most famous instances of this in literary history – Don Quixote setting off on chivalric adventures, Emma Bovary dreaming of chivalrous lovers – demonstrate the dangers of self-projection. Reality cedes to fantasy, so Cervantes and Flaubert show us, because the latter is more malleable, more amenable to flattering our fragile self-image. Many is the moment that I have consoled myself, after offending someone through an excess of candour, that I am a Nietzschean truthteller, uncowed by bourgeois niceties. Yet the banal reality is that I have simply offended someone. No amount of culture replaces tact.

From Plato onwards, critics of imaginative literature have seized on its ability to encourage over-identification, depicting fiction as a kind of decadent distortion of austere, incorruptible fact. The truth is, though, that the imagination only ever has purchase *as* imagination – as a supplement to, rather than a replacement for, lived experience. Collapse the distinction between fact and fiction and neither retains its meaning. Even when reading the most vividly conceived of stories, it is important to remember that in a very literal sense it is not about you.

But then literature itself can teach us this, if only we are paying attention. One of the great moral movements of literature is from self-obsession to self-suppression: protagonists attain insight because they become capable, finally, of looking outwards, of looking beyond themselves. In *Middlemarch*, for instance, Dorothea comes to realise that her interest in Casaubon was in fact self-interest, in the 'large vistas and wide fresh air which she had dreamed of finding in her husband's mind', only to see them replaced by 'ante-rooms and winding passages which seemed to lead nowhither'. She had been projecting her own needs and desires onto her choice of husband, she now recognises, rather than seeing him clearly for who he is. By the closing words of the novel, Dorothea's moral development is signalled by a shift in spatial metaphor. Her character is now described in terms of a river that 'spent itself in channels which had no great name on the earth. But the effect of her being on those around her was incalculably diffusive: for the growing good of the world is partly dependent on unhistoric acts.'

Here as elsewhere, Eliot is at pains to stress the open-ended selflessness of true character: no reward is expected, no return can be calculated. The word we use for this in everyday life, for that disinterested concern for the happiness of others that we reserve for close friends and family members, is love. Parental love, in particular, exemplifies those 'unhistoric acts' that Eliot extols, the many minor sacrifices – financial, emotional, physical – that children demand. We don't do things for them because we expect some return; we don't use them as the means to an end. We simply want them to thrive. Parental love is the very definition (or it should be) of what Kant calls the 'kingdom of ends', in which we treat everyone on their own terms and not as grist to our will.

Can we hope to extend this love to the world more generally? Such was the childless Eliot's ambition for art, the role of which, she wrote in an essay of 1856, is 'to amplify experience and extend our contact with our fellow-men beyond the bounds of our personal lot'. It might be *our* ambition, too: to extend our empathy with the world, with the aid of imaginative writing, beyond the bounds of our limited experience. The growing good of the world is dependent on cultivating not just our gardens, but our imagination.

For all our tendency to 'identify' with the protagonists of novels, we must also learn – just as they themselves must – that sometimes we need to dial down the narcissism. Identification, like identity politics, can be a trap, inviting us to see our own shadow rather than the outline of others. Distance, rather than proximity, is what helps us see further;

aesthetic education is also ethical education. In the kingdom of make-believe, we can be male or female, rich or
poor, alive or dead. In the imagination, we contain multitudes. It was because he was both man and woman, living
and unliving, that Tiresias became the moral centre of
T.S. Eliot's epoch-making poem, *The Waste Land* (1922).
Echoing the film *Spartacus*, when we read we can all say:
'I'm Tiresias.'

Helping us to adopt this multiple perspective is one of
the principal roles of books. It can also, of course, be one
of the principal roles of friends: my running group, with its
range of backgrounds and nationalities, ages and opinions,
forces me out of my bubble, warms up the tepid temperature
of male friendship. The problem, however, is that we tend
to stay in our bubbles, gravitating towards people who share
our education and interests. The views of our friends are all
too familiar.

Art, on the other hand, confronts us with the unfamil-
iar. In plays of the 1920s and 1930s such as *The Threepenny
Opera*, the German playwright Bertolt Brecht developed what
he termed a 'defamiliarisation effect', the aim of which was
to create, rather than collapse, the distance between audience
and art. 'Epic theatre', as Brecht's dramatic technique became
known, was intended to point to the world beyond the stage,
as well as to that on it, to induce reflection on our own position as well as on that of the characters in the play. Brecht's
agenda, as an avowed Marxist, was explicitly political. He
wanted to make us stand back from the action and reflect on

the socio-economic context of the events portrayed, on the vanishingly few alternatives available to Mack the Knife and his gang of pimps and prostitutes in the ill-starred Weimar Republic. Few of us, presumably, are ever likely to be in their position, yet Brecht helps us to imagine – and just as importantly, to *examine* – how they have come to find themselves where they do. Estranged from ourselves, we are forced to think as well as to feel.

We don't need to be fully paid-up Marxists to see that Brecht was onto something. Too often, identification with literary figures encourages complacency. We share Hamlet's tendency to indecisiveness, for instance, therefore we don't stop to think about the princely privileges that make it possible. To refuse identification, to impede empathy, is paradoxically empowering. It allows us to adopt a kind of Kantian disinterest whereby we do not necessarily take the hero's side – which means, by extension, that we do not necessarily take our own side. The advantages of this are obvious: critical distance not just from others but from ourselves, from our own assorted prejudices and presuppositions. By showing us that we are not at the centre of everything, aesthetics can help prepare us for politics and ethics.

'In the kingdom of make-believe, we can be male or female, rich or poor, alive or dead.'

Commandment three, then, is to learn to see things through the eyes of others. In the struggle between yourself and the world, declares Kafka, back the world. The more we read of other people's experiences and cultures, the more we challenge our own assumptions; the more we put on those tinted spectacles, the more we escape the prison of our own perspective. We can never completely escape our own consciousness, and would we even want to? But we can, at least, complement it with alternative ways of thinking. To make believe, in short, is to make space for others.

IV

Change your mind

Lesson four: Imagine other angles

LIKE MANY PEOPLE, I never leave the house without a magic box in my bag. Whenever I am feeling bored of life (how often we are bored of life!), whenever I am waiting for a train or wondering what to do with myself, there is always one easy thing that I can do: pull out the box. One of the single most addictive items of technology ever invented, the stimulation that it offers is inexhaustible, since life is inexhaustible. A simulacrum of sentiment, a virtual vademecum, the box always has something new to offer. The man who is tired of the magic box – if not of Dr Johnson's fateful phrase – is tired of life.

I might, perhaps, be talking about a telephone or an iPad. But I am, of course, referring to books. Magic books can be anything and everything. They can be a sanctuary or a challenge, a magnifying glass or a telescope. They can make us feel bigger or smaller, they can scale us up or scale us down. One thing they invariably do, though, is change our minds, in both the colloquial sense of making us think differently and the literal sense of altering our neural wiring. Through being reminded of the moral and aesthetic example of others, through imagining other people's imagined perspectives, we grow beyond our own spheres of influence, we learn about cultures and mentalities foreign to our native experience. If lesson two was that we must find our own narrative story, and lesson three that we must respect the right of others to do the same, lesson four is that we can change our minds simply by reading the words on a page.

When did you last change your mind? On the big questions in life – politics, religion, cultural identity – most of us form our ideas early and stick to them. We point our compass in one direction and keep going, disregarding, if necessary, all indications to the contrary. We may occasionally allow ourselves to have 'been wrong' about someone, but in truth this happens all too rarely; more often, experience teaches us what (we think) we already knew. Outside seminar rooms – perhaps inside seminar rooms – the unforced force of the better argument, in the phrase of the German philosopher Jürgen Habermas, rarely dissuades us from our own argument. Confirmation bias is the most human of prejudices.

I wish I could say I were different, but of course I cannot. I am as prone as the next person to repetition compulsion, to looking for the same thing in people, places and products – that thing, naturally, being mostly myself. 'When a man is attempting to describe another's character,' wrote the twenty-four-year-old Samuel Taylor Coleridge in 1796, 'he may be right or he may be wrong – but in one thing he will always succeed, in describing himself.' Even as I cite Coleridge, I am confirming his thesis, since I cite him to prove myself right. Solipsism insinuates itself into everything we do: to a greater or lesser extent we are all hostage to our own sense of self, to the many minor ways in which we feel good or bad about ourselves. It has always been said of Donald Trump, to take the most egregious example of such a hostage, that he has no sense of humour, because to have a sense of humour would be to acknowledge the existence of others. Confirming our mind is so much easier than changing it.

'Reading reminds us'

How can we address this? One way is to keep on reading, since reading re-minds us – that there are other perspectives, other ways of thinking and being. Not every piece of writing has the power to effect such changes, nor do we all respond to the same texts in the same ways. One man's balm is another man's banality; one woman's high art is another woman's low kitsch. One of the surest markers of true artistic achievement, though, is that it produces a psychological, indeed almost a physiological reaction in the reader. 'Although we read with our minds,' suggests Nabokov, 'the seat of artistic delight is between the shoulder blades [. . .] Let us worship the spine and its tingle.' Where Descartes held that the meeting-point of mind and matter was in the pineal gland, for Nabokov it is in the shoulder blades. To change our minds, we must listen to our bodies.

Even the most intellectual of existences, after all, is nothing if not embodied. We are not brains in a vat, as a famous philosophical problem of the 1980s posited; we perceive through our senses as well as through our thoughts. Emotion itself, as Nabokov implies, is an embodied experience, tingling through our spines as much as through our minds. One of the defining characteristics of language is that it is not *merely* language, since words are not merely empty signifiers. Numerous experiments have demonstrated the sense of satisfaction produced by the act of swearing, for instance: a combination of four otherwise arbitrary letters can create an emotional payoff – try saying 'fuck' gently – well in excess of their intellectual content. The same is true of literature, which has the capacity to produce psychological responses simply through the manipulation of linguistic markers. Shakespeare moves us through his mastery of metaphor; Austen amuses us through her mystery of humour. The change of mind that good writing effects is corporeal as well as cognitive.

It does not just change us in one direction, however. Literature chastens as much as it cheers. By situating us in a pre-existing tradition, by placing our concerns in a broader context, it amplifies our existence while gently rebuking our self-obsession. 'Humility is endless', wrote T.S. Eliot; more often than not, though, it is *beginning*-less, tied as we are to our insuperable egos. Sometimes in life we need to see ourselves as part of something bigger, even if this also makes us feel smaller. 'Greatness', the encounter with great writing or great art – with all its accumulated baggage, for us in the twenty-first century, of prejudice and predisposition – makes us aware of our own littleness, our own unimportance. It produces what Ezra Pound calls 'that sense of sudden growth which we experience in the presence of the greatest works of art'. Art changes our minds by changing our scale.

Part of this power, not the least significant part, lies in convincing us that we can legitimately respond to art in the first place. I see all the time in students, particularly those with little or no experience of sustained reading, the dawning realisation that these difficult texts with which they are grappling do in fact speak to them, and have something valid and interesting to say. The demands that reading makes on them – on *us* – are a drag until they are a draw. Serious interest in serious literature is a serious business. It can be difficult and draining, it can make sustained and often unreasonable claims on our powers of analysis and concentration. But it also *develops* our powers of analysis and concentration. Friends and family members often remark on my ability to sit reading amid a welter of other distractions, and also often remark on the pretentiousness – or even pointlessness – of doing so in the first place. Yet this does not diminish the importance of the endeavour. We have to *want* to expand our minds, just as we have to want to go to a museum or a church. Concentration is part of the challenge. A difficulty is a light, writes the French poet Paul Valéry; an insurmountable difficulty is a sun. To change our minds, first we have to challenge them.

'We can avoid making up our mind by making up our minds.'

One way of doing this is to make up our minds – not in the decisive sense of fixing on a particular meaning, but in the inventive sense of creating fictional meanings. The Portuguese polific writer Fernando Pessoa takes this tendency to its logical extreme, inventing dozens of *noms de plume* or 'homonyms' and ascribing whole biographies and back stories to them. Ricardo Reis is a classicist, Alberto Caeiro a pastoral poet, Álvaro de Campos a worldly man of letters: none of them are Fernando Pessoa, and all of them are Fernando Pessoa. 'Each of us is several, is many, is a profusion of selves', writes Bernardo Soares, yet another of the Lisbon author's alter egos. Of whom is this not true? None of us is the same person day after day, nor should we want to be; no one is consistent with themselves over the course of their entire lifetime. As Pessoa shows us, we can avoid making up our mind by making *up* our minds.

Another way of saying this is that literature amplifies our petty concerns by projecting them, like the shadows in Plato's cave, onto a broader canvas. The more widely we read and think, the more colour we have to paint onto the canvas. The allusions gathered in these essays are themselves a modest example of the power of literature to give us purpose. It is not just that we are what we read – we *become* what we read. 'I am only slightly exaggerating', writes Rilke in 1909, in one of his many lyrical letters exploring the meaning of life, 'when I say that we *are* not; we are constantly forming ourselves anew and different in the intersection of all the influences that impact on our lives.' The greater the range of influences, it follows, the greater the intersection. The more promiscuous the reading, the better. If we all exist at the centre of our own Venn diagram, it makes sense to broaden the circles around us as much as possible.

If art is supremely good at helping us do this, it is because the circles move in both directions, both away from us and back to us. This ebb and flow is what the humanities can offer: not so much a morality lesson – all those SS officers reading Goethe after a hard day's murdering quickly dispel this notion – as a psychology lesson. We are not better people when we read attentively (we might be worse), but we are *broader* people, more exposed to other influences. In this, of course, reading is like travelling, a passport to new perspectives.

I changed my own mind most conclusively when I spent six months, in my early twenties, on a tropical island in the Indian Ocean. Ostensibly there to study French, I spent more time on the beach than in the classroom, swimming with brightly coloured fish and reading under luxuriant palm trees. No doubt it sounds like a holiday, but it was more, in fact, like a chrysalis, a transitional period out of which emerged a mature, adult sensibility. The distance from my previous life was psychological as well as physical. Marooned with Joyce and Dante, exiled with Baudelaire and Dickinson, I read my way into being a different, more capacious person. The experience was decisive, determining the direction of my development ever since, pulling me into purpose as I returned to the mainland. Stepping out of my life, if only temporarily, allowed me to step back into it.

'Literature helps us approach the Medusa of our minds at one remove.'

The psychological value of such distance is incalculable, not least because in our daily doings we tend to avoid confronting our fears and failings head-on. In the rueful words of T.S. Eliot, when reflecting on *The Use of Poetry and the Use of Criticism* (1933), 'our lives are mostly a constant evasion of ourselves'. Literature helps avoid the evasion by offering us ersatz emotions – pity, laughter, satisfaction, frustration – to supplement our own. If other people's problems are easier to adjudicate, so too are other people's emotions, since we have no stake in evading them. We gain a flash of recognition – a moment of *anagnorisis* – as we suddenly see that we, too, share a given character's temperament, whether Hamlet's prevarication or Raskolnikov's misanthropy. Yet this is only possible because we are not looking directly at our own short-comings, but at a reflected version of them. Like Perseus's shield, literature helps us approach the Medusa of our minds at one remove.

In literature as in life, the challenge comes when the Gorgon starts to age. It is all very well forming your tastes and discovering yourself through books when young, but what happens when you reach middle age and realise that you are now set in your ways? Is it possible, or even desirable, to *keep* changing your mind? Balding men and worrying women, limping creatures of time and circumstance, can we resist our own biology? One way to do so is to refine our psychology, to re-read the books that meant so much to us when younger to see whether they look the same now we are older. Another way is to seek out different kinds of books, different kinds of cultures from the ones we already know: non-European, for instance, or pre-modern literature (the ageing Goethe turned to both when he began rewriting Hafiz in his sixties). To be the same person at fifty as at twenty would be unconscionable, but prejudice and presupposition stalk both ages just the same. Only an open mind can be changed.

The most striking examples of how writing changes minds occur, inevitably, in a religious context. In his *Confessions* (c. AD 400), for instance, Saint Augustine recounts how, at the age of thirty-one, he discovered God. Prompted by a child's voice to 'take up and read' – *tolle lege!* – he opened the Bible at random and came across Paul's Epistle to the

Figure 4: '*Tolle lege!*' Philippe de Champaigne,
Saint Augustine, c. 1650

Romans, more specifically the section describing the 'transformation of believers' from the law of Moses to the grace of God. Augustine took this as a sign to change his dissolute ways, and was baptised the following year.

Such moments of complete conversion are surpassingly rare, and they mark the boundary at which literature becomes religion. But literature can also become life: 'take up and read' applies to us all, if only we acknowledge the imperative. Our horizons, whether intellectual, moral or emotional, are much broader than we think; we just have to be *prepared* to think. Preparation, in the scientific sense, is what good writing offers us, a distillation of elements designed to produce a particular response, that tell-tale tingle in the shoulder blades. This can, of course, cut both ways. A well-written sentence or a felicitous form of words can capture our imagination for better or for worse; sophistry and rhetoric serve both activism and fascism. Used as a force for good, though, words can change the world. If many of the major writers of the nineteenth century, such as Dickens, Zola and Hugo, were also major activists and campaigners, it is because they knew how to turn a phrase. '*J'accuse!*' is nothing if not an arresting formulation.

We all stand accused of ignorance one way or another, and reading is one of the supreme ways to mitigate it. The problem, though, is that we tend to seek out perspectives that reinforce our own; in literature as in life, we are attracted to what we already know. Literary tradition, like social media, risks being an echo chamber that plays back to us our pre-existing prejudices. Such are the stakes of the culture wars, the struggle over who gets to say what does and does not constitute our cultural inheritance. For if we merely read the usual litany of white Western men, how will we ever develop any new perspectives? The question applies equally, of course, to our daily lives. If we only see the same people, how will we make space for genuine difference, for the authentically new? Do we even want it?

Changing our mind – altering the way that we think – is the challenge of true aesthetic experience precisely because we *don't* always want it. Incessant challenge is intolerable; as we get older in particular, it is much easier to stick than to twist.

Czesław Miłosz, the Polish poet who survived both fascism and communism and knew a thing or two about the relationship between life and literature, noted in his study *The Captive Mind* (1953) that he would often think of 'how like a smooth slope any form of art is, and of the amount of effort the artist must expend in order to keep from sliding back to where the footing is easier'. The problem is pressing for all of us, even if we haven't won the Nobel prize or lived in a murderous dictatorship. How do we keep moving up the slope?

Perhaps the answer is to change slope. To choose a new challenge, to begin again, is the great dream of middle age. Unless we undergo a religious epiphany or political volte-face, however, it is difficult to change our beliefs completely. Incremental alterations are far more attainable, and it is here that art, and in particular literature, with its ability to reflect discursively on its own premises, can be so helpful. Every book I read, every book I write, changes my mind in some small way, in part because it makes me aware of aspects of my mind that I didn't realise needed changing in the first place. Learning new languages – and reading in these languages – reveals new facets of our personality; whenever I am in Paris or Stuttgart, I am conscious that I am a subtly different person, the sum total of my subtly different experiences in French or in German. The so-called Sapir-Whorf hypothesis of twentieth-century linguistics (the idea, named after the two scientists associated with it, that linguistic structure pre-determines cognitive perception) holds true for us all: our language – and thus also, our literature – influences how we see the world. Words are a mind-altering substance.

Unlike drugs, however, with their rapid transition from rush to remorse, reading changes us for ever. Who thinks of life in the trenches in the same way having read Remarque, or the war poets? Who can unsee the horror, the horror of Western colonialism having read *Heart of Darkness*? And it is not just historical events or periods that literature inflects. Our experience of even abstract, metaphysical phenomena such as time or pity can never be the same once we have considered them through the eyes of Marcel Proust or George Eliot – not to mention romantic love, coloured as it is by the star-crossed clichés of *Romeo and Juliet*. The more we read, the more sensitive our perceptual filters become. To paraphrase Portia, the quality of mercy is not strained – it is refined.

'Language influences how we see the world.
Words are a mind-altering substance.'

To be in two minds – and to be able to switch between these two minds – is an invaluable life skill, and it is one that literature is ideally placed to enable. First articulated in 1817, Keats's notion of 'negative capability' – to be 'capable of being in uncertainties, Mysteries, doubts, without any irritable reaching after fact & reason' – offers an object lesson in the capacity of imaginative writing for such open-mindedness. *Not* to have a fixed view on something is a rare ability, one much prized by leaders and decision makers, since it makes it possible to listen to advice dispassionately and without prejudice before reaching a balanced conclusion. Barack Obama, for instance, has repeatedly talked about the importance of reading to inform his sensibility, noting in a conversation of 2015 with Marilynne Robinson that 'the most important stuff I've learned I think I've learned from novels. It has to do with empathy. It has to do with being comfortable with the notion that the world is complicated and full of grays, but there's still truth there to be found, and that you have to strive for that and work for that.' Literary fiction offers negative capability beyond the reach of historical fact.

It is up to all of us, whether world leaders or not, to cultivate a mind that is informed but open to change. This is no small challenge. The Keynesian cliché that 'when the facts change, I change my mind' is memorable because it is so rare. To be wrong, psychologically, is harder than we like to admit: three years on from the enactment of Brexit, what is astonishing is not that *some* people have changed their mind, but that so many more have *not*, despite all the evidence as to its harm. Most of us, most of the time, reach a position on something – Brexit, Boris Johnson, God – and then stick to it, irrespective of evidence to the contrary. Nietzsche is surely closer to the mark than Keynes when he records the all too brief struggle between truth and pride – at the end of which, with crushing inevitability, truth gives way. Human minds cannot bear very much reality.

It is in this context that literature, with its ability to reinvent the real, can play such a vital role. It functions, in essence, like those apps that transform photographs into cartoons, transporting reality into the realm of the imagination with one small shift. Art does not aspire to 'truth', but to emotional insight. It does not pretend to tell us how things actually were – to borrow Aristotle's enduring distinction between history and literature – but how things *might* be. The imagination is driven by the subjunctive, not the indicative, by all those conditionals and counterfactuals that offer alternative visions of how to live and love, laugh and cry. Art is aspirational emotionally as well as intellectually.

It can only be so, though, because it shows us where we are not (yet) getting things right. One of the standard questions at job interviews, common to many professions, is to share an occasion on which you got something wrong. It's tricky to answer, of course, since you want to show humility without humiliation, to show that you have learned something from failure while laying the foundation for future success. Reading can help us answer this question in a more interesting way, since it can help us see when we have got something wrong. If not Dostoevsky's Grand Inquisitor, literature is a great indicator of shortfalls in our imaginative engagement with the world. Before reading Rousseau, I had never considered what it meant to 'return to nature'; before reading Dickens, I had never considered what it meant to live as an orphan in a workhouse. To shift our point of view on something, to help us imagine other angles, is the measure of imaginative success. 'What else is our métier', writes Rilke in another of his meditative letters, 'than creating opportunities for change?'

To change your mind is a mark of strength, not of weakness, since it is a mark of enduring incipience. If literature can help us retain this incipience – the ability to begin again, and again and again – it is because it leads us to *think* differently as well as to think *differently*. Both verb and adverb require emphasis, since reading affects both conceptual beliefs and cognitive style. Having read a given author or text, we may now hold changed views on politics or society, but we may also now phrase those views in changed terms – in short, staccato sentences like Hemingway, or in long, stately sentences like Proust. *What* we think might change, but so might *how* we think – and how we think, as the Sapir-Whorf hypothesis suggests, is as important as what we think, since it makes it possible in the first place. As the German author Heinrich von Kleist despairingly concluded when he read Kant at the start of the nineteenth century (leading him, ultimately, to shoot himself in 1811): if we are wearing green glasses then the world looks green. Our style colours our substance, our adverbs our verbs; aesthetics predetermines ethics. The magic box plays tricks on the brain.

Poetry makes nothing happen, Auden claimed. But poetry does make something happen: it changes our minds.

V

Discover your own language

Lesson five: Find your name, find your voice

NAMING – the solemn declaration that a certain combination of letters will henceforth constitute the marker of our identity – is one of the first and most important things that happens to us during our lifetimes. Its symbolic value is enormous, locking us into a whole host of codes whether we like them or not. From class and religion to gender and generation, names are nothing if not predetermined by association. Conferred on us without our consent, they impose a certain vision of who our parents would like us to be. One of our earliest encounters with language is the stammering attempt to learn our own names, as though they really were our *own* and not given. Even if we choose to change our name in later life, as people sometimes do, this very act merely confirms its representative force. *Nomen est omen*, as the old tag has it. Nothing defines us more than our name.

It is no surprise that naming is also one of the earliest acts of literature. In its Old Testament origins, language confers meaning with an almost magical force. God names Adam, Adam names the beasts: 'and whatsoever Adam called every living creature, that *was* the name thereof' (Genesis 2:18). Language, *logos*, determines humankind's relationship to life from the start. By the time of the New Testament, naming had become a central concern of Christianity; indeed in some ways it *is* Christianity, since to christen is, of course, to name. In the beginning was the Word: John baptises Jesus, and the Bible christens Western culture with symbolic purpose. From a different perspective, meanwhile, Judaism is equally emphatic about the importance of naming. 'Yahweh', the name of God, is too holy to be vocalised, an unpronounceable string of consonants – Yod, Heh, Vav and Heh (YHWH) – subsumed, for fear of offending the Almighty, into the placeholder 'Adonai'. Thousands of years later, the best-selling book since the Bible confirms the edict: in the world of Harry Potter, 'He who cannot be named' is the very incarnation of evil. From antiquity to modernity, names have lost none of their incantatory power.

'A name is a story in miniature.'

Writers know what they are doing, then, when they invoke the metaphysics of nomenclature. From Shakespeare to Melville, from Dickens to Joyce, the creation of evocative names has long been a test of genius, akin to Leonardo da

Vinci's alleged ability to draw a perfect circle freehand. For a name is a story in miniature, a fictional conceit to which we acquiesce and attribute any manner of ideas and implications. 'Call me Ishmael': in three pithy words, the opening imperative of Hermann Melville's *Moby-Dick* (1851) brings a whole character to life. Melville's choice of name is, of course, far from accidental: just as the biblical Ishmael wandered the desert, so the fictional Ishmael will wander the seas. But the choice of verb concedes the essential arbitrariness of fiction – *let's pretend to* call our protagonist Ishmael – while at the same time invoking its creative, non-arbitrary power. The self-generating ability of fiction, its capacity to call itself into consciousness, recalls nothing so much as the inveterate exaggerator Baron Munchhausen's tall tale, in Rudolf Erich Raspe's book of 1785, of emerging from the swamp by pulling himself up by his own hair. Naming, like writing, is not so much a confidence trick as a conjuring trick, summoning characters – and character – out of thin air.

How do we summon our own character? By discovering, I want to suggest, our own language. I do not mean by this that we should all try to create a new Esperanto or literary masterpiece (as if we were even capable of it). What I am advocating, rather, is that we should all seek our natural idiom. 'Owning' the way in which we speak and write, the way we dress and move, is an important step towards owning our lives. To own is to take responsibility, and to take responsibility is to take control. Find your own tone, runs the standard advice given to aspiring writers; find your own voice. If it does nothing

Münchhausen   O. Herrfurth pinx

Figure 5: Pulling himself up by his own name:
Oskar Herrfurth, *Baron von Münchhausen*

else, art shows us that aesthetic identity is also existential identity. Human consciousness, in the words of Wallace Stevens, is in perpetual pursuit of a language and a style.

It takes time to find our own language and style. We're all trying to work out who we are: the search accelerates in adolescence and decelerates in maturity, but it never settles. I thought I had figured myself out by early adulthood. I wanted to live the life of the mind, as intentionally as possible; I wanted to use words, as purposefully as possible. This hasn't changed, but its expression has. Somewhere along the line – when I 'grew up'? when I had children? – my yearning for complexity became a longing for clarity. Part of this is learning to see through the bullshit, the emperor's new prose of a thousand intellectual poseurs. Impressionable, intellectually ambitious students are particularly susceptible to this kind of jargon; I know because I was one, although thankfully I retained my native scepticism. To a self-conscious adolescent, 'cool' means making things harder, withholding meaning. To a self-conscious adult, it means making things simpler, *holding* meaning, stripping away the accretions of chic and circumstance. Or perhaps it means recognising that there is *only* circumstance – that our task is not so much to follow it as to rub against it, to spark ourselves into independence. We are in search not just of purpose, but of our own way of *articulating* purpose.

In this regard, as in so many others, literature is a forcing house for life. Just as writers create characters, so we too compete for naming rights in the arena of our own existence.

'Civilisation consists in giving something a name that doesn't belong to it and then dreaming over the result', suggests Pessoa, writing under one of his many false names. 'And the false name joined to the true dream does create a new reality. The object does change into something else, because we make it change. We manufacture realities.' It is not just writers who make believe: all of us, all the time, manufacture realities. Like children, we have 'given' names, but we also want to *give* names; like Adam, we are given voice, but we also want to *give* voice. We are all seeking both our own language and our own sense of agency and identity, and this is something that the creative fiat of literature – 'A voice comes to one in the dark. Imagine.' (to quote Beckett) – is uniquely placed to encourage. How can we find our own words?

Through the words of others, might be the paradoxical answer. Literature teaches us the basic existential lesson that self-determination requires learning not just from ourselves, but from others – and that this relationship to others, for humans, is necessarily linguistic. To be human is to be what the Canadian philosopher Charles Taylor calls 'the language animal': words are our superpower, our point of difference, both cause and effect of our unique evolutionary path. Human culture is nothing if not linguistic, for it is founded on the ability to give names to things both real and imagined.

While the supreme manifestation of such ability lies in literature, in the quasi-miraculous creation of characters and consciousness *ex nihilo*, even those of us who don't create characters create our own character. We are all imagining ourselves all the time, pulling ourselves up by our own hair through sheer force of conviction. The strands of self-confidence are fragile, though, which is why we look to others for reassurance and guidance. The danger is that we get tangled up trying to please these others, that we try too hard to live up to predetermined expectations. Matthew Arnold's much-contested definition of culture as the 'best that has been thought and said' was first proposed in the late 1860s, and represents a high-water mark of Western self-confidence. His unselfconscious assumption of degrees of quality – that certain cultural achievements simply *are* the best, irrespective of changing historical conditions and criteria – may jar in our post-imperial era, but for the same reason it captures our quandary in the twenty-first century. How might we mere mortals, chastened creatures of a lesser age, live up to such lofty claims? How can individuals escape the burden of tradition?

'We are all imagining ourselves all the time,
pulling ourselves up by our own hair.'

The only way to do so, in the end, is to find our own voice. That it is banal and belated does not diminish its legitimacy, since it is the *assertion* of autonomy that matters, not its quality. Literature can teach us this much: Shakespeare, to cite its supreme embodiment, is never more moving than when he abjures rough magic in favour of raw modesty. Prospero's closing envoi in *The Tempest* – 'what strength I have's mine own, / which is most faint' – asserts the claims of authenticity over majesty in a kind of self-fulfilling paradox, through which faintness *becomes* strength precisely because it is given voice. To admit one's weakness is to control it. True liberty lies not in tricks and charms, but in the steadfast appraisal of one's own (necessarily limited) capacities. Ability requires vulnerability.

Vulnerability is fashionable for the modern male, the long-overdue backlash against millennia of masculinity. That doesn't make it any easier to accept. For all the exhortations to emote, for all the podcasts about the paternal condition in the twenty-first century, I was raised to be sovereign of my sentiments. Encouraged to project strength and self-sufficiency, I struggle not to impose such strictures on my own children, not to tell them to get a grip on their mercurial emotions. A parody of a middle-class parent, I tell my boys to mark their 'I's and floss their 't's, to mimic the master's voice. But they need to find their own voice, not mine; they need to find their own grammar of feeling. I can't, I shouldn't, control them.

Books can help both me and them with this, since books give direct access to the brain, unmediated by external authority. Relinquishing control, in this regard, is easier read than done. We can't internalise all emotion; we can, however, internalise meaning. We can internalise our own relationship to the world, our own way of situating ourselves within an otherwise alien environment. Children know this, eagerly naming pets, cars, toys as a way of establishing a personal, proprietorial link to them. Naming is taming: we bind the world to us through the spell of language. But the spell works both ways, since others do the same to us. The idea of declaring 'permitted pronouns' at the end of email signatures can be understood in this light, as a way of reasserting control of one's own linguistic markers. Identity politics, if they are anything, are also language politics.

'Naming is taming: we bind the world to us through the spell of language.'

Another way of saying this is that naming constitutes what language philosophers call a 'performative' act. In the standard example of such an act – 'I hereby declare you husband and wife' – it is the making of the statement that enacts the claim: the state of being married is called into existence through its very pronouncement. The same is true, quite obviously, of naming. 'I hereby call you Ishmael' is both a declaration and an action, indeed the declaration *is* the action.

This becomes more than merely trivial if we look at Melville's opening paragraphs. They are defined by a particular class of performatives, namely imperatives. The famous first sentence of *Moby-Dick* is an especially striking example of the genre. Through the simple assertion of (his own) identity, the narrator – himself, of course, a fictitious conceit – makes himself both subject and object of the reader's attention, jump-starting himself into being through a kind of syntactical sleight of hand. He does not say 'I hereby call *you* Ishmael', but rather 'I hereby call *myself* Ishmael'. Melville finds both name and voice at the same time.

We're all trying to do this, since we all want to be the subject and object of our own existence. We want to feel not just in control, but in *creative* control of our lives. Anyone who has ever been tempted to change their name, perhaps during adolescence, knows the feeling: the yearning to be someone else, to inhabit some other kind of identity. Who hasn't found their own life boring or limited? Children play by imagining themselves as someone else, by giving themselves names – I'll be Mbappé, you be Messi – that confer a larger, bolder identity. In French, children even use the conditional tense – I *would be* Mbappé, you *would be* Messi – enacting the very act of imagination it implies. At times, no doubt, we would all be someone else.

Art helps us to retain into adulthood this adolescent urge for self-fashioning. It helps us direct our attention, as the opening chapter of *Moby-Dick* does through a string of imperatives – Go! Look! Say! – towards the pull of the sea. For this, Ishmael tells us, is what artists do, compelling our gaze towards the oceanic feeling within us beyond the merely mundane. Ishmael's imperatives enact his evocation of the ocean as the great other to our landlocked lives: *evoking* is quite literally what they do, giving voice to the 'image of the ungraspable phantom of life; and this is the key to it all'. To name is to write; to write is to dream; to dream is to transcend our common concerns, to give our humdrum lives greater depth and reach. Such is the aim both of Melville's self-starting narrator, and of literature itself: to broaden our landlocked lives.

'We all want to be the subject and object
of our own existence.'

Of the many picaresque names in *Moby-Dick* – Captain Ahab, the boat *Pequod* – the most celebrated is, no doubt, that of the whale itself. Melville's disquisition in Chapter 45 on four other famous whales reflects the importance of being 'admitted into all the rights, privileges, and distinctions of a name'. Watch them surface, those legendary leviathans: Timor Jack, 'scarred like an iceberg'; New Zealand Tom, 'terror of all cruisers'; Morquan, 'King of Japan'; and Don Miguel, 'marked like an old tortoise with mystic hieroglyphics upon the back'. All four creatures, Melville remarks, are 'as well known to the students of Cetacean History as Marius or Scylla to the classic scholar'. Naming, in other words – or rather, in those *particular* words – confers identity and speci-ficity, raising the status of the animals from *a* whale to *that* whale. Ahab, like Adam, names the beasts in order to tame the beasts.

The idea that the name or well-chosen word provides the 'key to it all' is one of the recurring lessons of literary history. Instances of it are legion in the literatures of the world: uttered as an imperative – 'Open Sesame!' – it is at times quite literally a key, assuming an almost tautological force (what does the imperative add?) that serves to underline the power of the password. The magic name as uttered in the *Arabian Nights* echoes the use of such terms in Judaeo-Christian culture, perhaps most fatefully in the episode of the 'shibboleth' in the Book of Judges. When the Ephraimites attempted to return home across the River Jordan after their defeat in battle, their enemies the Gileadites asked each of them to say the word (which originally designated an ear of corn). If they could not pronounce it properly – they would say 'sibboleth', owing to their inability to pronounce the 'sh' sound – they were slaughtered where they stood. Having the right voice became a life-or-death matter.

It is also, less dramatically, a meaning-of-life matter. How can we live fully if we don't express ourselves fully? Learning to use language purposefully – to say what *we* want to say, not what everyone around us is saying – is one of the great life tasks, and it is not one that all of us master. Education helps, but it also hinders, since we come to conform to the codes and models of our masters (in a way exemplified by accent, as an inherited rather than chosen way of speaking). Emancipation, whether verbal, political or ethical, must in the end be on our own terms. One way of establishing these terms is to learn a *new* language (or accent) and so to become, to whatever extent, a new person. I see this with my boys. Blessed with bilingualism, they bounce not only between English and French but between different versions of themselves, between different ways of expressing who they are or want to be. The mistakes and misunderstandings – not least culturally, since they don't always realise that what is appropriate in one language is inappropriate in another – are part of the project. Franglais (or Denglish, Spanglish, or any other hybrid) can be a voice of its own.

Finding this voice is the difference between fitting in and falling out, between living and dying – and between good or bad writing. If 'voice' is the holy grail, the Open Sesame, of any authentic text, it is because an original idiom discloses the world from an original angle. In this way it functions as an extended version of the power to name, of the power of language to give voice to mute experience. Such power is, of course, the essence of lyric poetry: the well-wrought term is the aim of all self-respecting poets. The Romantic tradition, with its attempt to enchant the world, makes that aim the very essence of its writing, as one of the pithiest poems in German demonstrates clearly. First published in 1838, the Romantic writer Joseph von Eichendorff's 'Divining Rod' (*Wünschelrute*) performs the very act it evokes:

> There's a song in all things ringing,
> Lost in dreams and still unheard.
> And the world breaks forth in singing
> When you find the magic word.

The magic word here is, of course, that of the poem itself. In a single, concise stanza, it brings the world to song through its incantatory rhythms, performing the thing it prescribes. Magic is in the melody: the divining rod – Melville's key – is the poet's pen. Language is life.

As Eichendorff's poem demonstrates, literature can help us to re-enchant a disenchanted world. Perhaps the best adjective for this lesson is 'Orphic': like the mythological figure of Orpheus, the poet gives voice to the dumb-show of life. The best-known Orphic poet of the modern era is undoubtedly Rilke, whose later work is premised on the very possibility of naming, saying and praising the 'interpreted world'. If his *Sonnets to Orpheus* (1922) enchant life into sound – 'Oh Orpheus sings! Oh great tree in the ear!' – his *Duino Elegies* (1912–22) clarify the stakes of such enchantment, and in terms that leave little doubt as to the main contribution of humanity to existence:

> Are we here perhaps *here* for the saying of: house,
> bridge, spring of water, gate, pitcher, fruit-tree, window –
> at the utmost: column, tower . . . but to *speak* them,
>   you understand,
> oh, to speak them in forms these Things themselves in
>   their heart
> never believed they would be.

Rilke, channelling Orpheus, identifies humans – and above all, poets – as the custodians of speech. Our nature is to name; our value is our voice, our ability to *give* voice to pitted, palpitating reality. 'Here is the time of the sayable', he concludes; '*here* its homeland. / Speak, and bear witness'.

To speak in such terms is, of course, the role of the writer. There is no reason to think, however, that it cannot also be an aim for the rest of us. We must not let the ideal be the enemy of the possible. Just because we are not as eloquent as Rilke, this doesn't mean that we don't have our own stories to tell; just because we are not poets, this doesn't mean that we can't find our own voice. The vernacular is as valid as the spectacular: everyday language, as writers such as Brontë or Joyce have long delighted in showing, can be as powerful as high style. We, too, can speak and bear witness. To find our voice, to put it in literary terms, is to find our *register*, our defining level of language. What are our childish attempts to scrawl our signature if not the first tentative assertions of sovereignty?

Sovereignty can only be acquired, though, through interaction with others. Our names are 'given' before they are taken. My boys Maximilien and Hugo – it is time that I gave them their names, their own identities – can only practise their signatures, with their tentative swirls and extravagant flourishes, because they have learned to master the common tongue. Without language, there is no *logos*; without words, there is no meaning, in both the semantic and spiritual senses of the term. We can only name ourselves, become ourselves, if we listen to others.

The true commandment, then, is not just to find your voice, but to open your ears. The true commandment is to communication. As Wittgenstein famously suggested, there can be no such thing as a private language – not just for intellectual, but also for emotional reasons, since naming implies needing. We give names to people, pets and things because we seek a relationship with them; we give voice to our concerns because we want others to hear them. It is no good finding your voice if there is no one there to hear it. With all its ingenuity in coining names and creating characters, with all its semantic subtlety, what literature ultimately teaches us is that no man, however self-sufficient, is an island. To find your voice, first you have to hear someone else's.

VI

Learn from the past

Lesson six: Escape the tyranny of now

THE PRESSURES OF LIFE in the twenty-first century are enormous. From climate change to pandemics, from refugee crises to the cost of living, the anxieties that assail us all are inescapable. Emails intrude on our every instant: constant connectivity brings constant concern, the wi-fi worries of an attention-deficit age. Doom-scrolling is one of the defining activities of the Western world: we are preoccupied, with good reason, by the urgency of the present, fixated on our contemporary problems. Eight billion people are crowded on our shrinking planet. How are we to avoid obsessing over them and doing nothing else?

One way to do so is to remember that they are a mere fraction of all the people who have ever lived. As of 2023, the Population Reference Bureau estimates the total population of human history at about 117 billion; this means that for every person living now, nearly fifteen have lived previously. Mathematically speaking, the past has a much larger claim on our attention than the present (as, of course, does the future, although the numbers for that are unavailable). Morally speaking, 'presentism' – the bias towards what is happening here and now – is untenable. Engaging with history is imperative.

It is here that the humanities can help. The humanities are sometimes criticised for focusing on the past rather than the present, yet it is this ability to escape the present that is precisely their strength. 'Tradition', wrote G.K. Chesterton in 1908, 'refuses to submit to the small and arrogant oligarchy of those who merely happen to be walking about. All democrats object to men being disqualified by the accident of birth; tradition objects to their being disqualified by the accident of death.' If culture is cumulative and egalitarian, amounting to what Chesterton terms 'a democracy of the dead', so too are our lives. Memory-driven mammals, we are the aggregate of everything that has been thought and said. Literature, the '*best* that has been thought and said', can help us learn from the trial and error of others by teaching us a kind of historical humility.

The idea has inhabited me since adolescence. Words from the past quicken the present, thicken it with a metaphysical lining. The meaninglessness of long stretches of my life has been mitigated by the meaning*ful*ness of books, by the sense that even while losing time I am gaining time, or perhaps regaining it in the Proustian sense. Hiding from the heat with little to do, the long summer holidays of my early twenties were the perfect occasion to read *In Search of Lost Time*, to be bored like Marcel, to languish like Marcel, to realise, like Marcel, that memory is what makes meaning possible. Purpose surprised me in the act of reading: having raised aimlessness to an art form – by God I was aimless, adrift in a sea of marijuana and misanthropy – Proust pointed to a way of redeeming it all, of giving shape and structure to my incoherent existence. His exquisite, interminable sentences were like my exquisite, interminable summers, equal parts ravishing and redundant. Drowsing over Proust for want of anything better to do is like living for want of anything better to do – with the twist that at the end, amazingly, it all makes sense, as the past catches up with the present in a sudden swoon of meaning. Only art can be this perfect, I said to myself, this is what I want to devote my life to doing, I said to myself: spending and regaining time.

Yet time is the one thing so few of us have. Between careers and children, chores and commuting, we rush from task to task, ever conscious of the tick behind the tock. How many of us have time to regain time? How many of us have time to read Proust? (Do people even aspire to this any more?) If Proust functions as the embodiment of the author 'we should have read', it's mainly because of the notorious length of his book, as though this alone makes him the ultimate marker of cultural prestige. But the real reason we should read him is that he doesn't make us lose time, but *regain* it; he makes us see that memory is what makes our lives cohere. Proust helps us realise that meaning is in our minds.

'The past presses upon us all with unquenchable clamour.'

I have spent many years since then chasing this moment of meaning. If I am still waiting for the epiphany, it is because it has dissolved into an ongoing process, the continuous projection of purpose implicit in Proust's title. Fugitive as it necessarily is, the attempt to corral and contain time is built not just into all artistic endeavour, but into how we understand the history of artistic endeavour. 'All ages are contemporaneous', in the words of Proust's contemporary Ezra Pound. 'This is especially true of literature, where the real time is independent of the apparent, and where many dead men are our grand-children's contemporaries.' The past presses upon us all with unquenchable clamour.

'Tradition' is the name we give to this clamour. The term is generally understood to mean conservative or unchanging – to be 'traditional' is to be old-fashioned – but there is no reason why this should automatically be the case. It simply depends on *which part* of a tradition one is advocating; like 'quality' or 'temper', the term has been reduced to one end of its spectrum of meanings. It is perfectly possible to adopt a traditional left-wing perspective, or a traditional Proustian point of view. That the adjective tends to the right-wing and pejorative – he is 'very traditional' – tells us as much about what the historian A.J.P. Taylor called the enormous condescension of posterity as it does about the person or perspective in question. To hand something down – the etymology of the term – is not to expect it to be unchanging.

The most famous of modern literary engagements with tradition suggests as much. Writing in 1919, Pound's protégé T.S. Eliot observed that 'if the only form of tradition, of handing down, consisted in following the ways of the immediate generation before us in a blind or timid adherence to its successes, "tradition" should positively be discouraged.' As he notes, however, the term implies considerably more:

> Tradition is a matter of much wider significance.
> It cannot be inherited, and if you want it you must
> obtain it by great labour. It involves, in the first
> place, the historical sense, which we may call nearly
> indispensable to anyone who would continue to be a
> poet beyond his twenty-fifth year; and the historical
> sense involves a perception, not only of the pastness
> of the past, but of its presence; the historical sense
> compels a man to write not merely with his own
> generation in his bones, but with a feeling that
> the whole of the literature of Europe from Homer
> and within it the whole of the literature of his own
> country has a simultaneous existence and composes
> a simultaneous order.

What Eliot calls the 'historical sense', I want to suggest, is indispensable to us all, individual talents or not. His claim that no poet can have 'complete meaning' alone is true, too, for the rest of us; we must all be 'set, for contrast and comparison, among the dead'. We don't just inherit the past; we have to earn it. History, culture, literature – reading Proust, remembering Homer – can be hard work.

It is also, very often, artwork. That the past is as fictional as it is factual is one of the key lessons of literature. Writers cultivate the simultaneous existence of the past with the present because they cultivate the simultaneous existence of the imagination with reality: that shimmering mirage 'then' hovers over the arid desert of 'now'. The past can *only* be imagined; every act of remembering is an act of re-creating, since time alters everything, including our own perspective on it. I remember first reading Eliot's essay, half a lifetime ago. Not yet 'beyond my twenty-fifth year', ambitious but unformed, I was intrigued, but hardly invested in his plea for the past, since I myself had so little of it. Twenty years later, Eliot's historical sense has become my own historical sense, my hazy recollection of how I understood 'tradition', on first encounter, as little more than a tedious list of texts and titles. I still find a good number of those texts and titles tedious, but I now see that they have value as part of an ongoing order, as a way of structuring our minds and softening our self-obsession. As citizens of the contemporary, we all need ways of avoiding recency bias.

Reading literature, as Eliot suggests, is one way to mitigate this bias. Through revisiting its imaginative interpretations, through remembering both its takes and its mistakes, we learn about and from the past. We tend to think of this as happening through the discipline of history – those who cannot remember the past are doomed to repeat it – but why can it not also happen through *literary* history? Creative writing is as instructive as any historical document, since it shows us not just how things were, but how we would have liked them to be. To read John Milton, for instance, is to learn not only about the Protestant mindset of Civil War England, but about what it *wanted* to be, about its impassioned invocation of uncensored thought and freedom of speech. To read Emily Dickinson is to feel, from the inside out, what it meant to be a monastic woman with metaphysical longings. What better way into the mind of a time than through its dreams?

Remembering our own dreams of the past, and our distance from them in the present, is one way of measuring our meaning. Few of us end up living exactly the way we had hoped to as we emerged from childhood. Even for those of us who do – Nobel prize winners, prime ministers? – the fulfilment of ambition never feels the same as its imagination, if only because we have all become different people along the way. On a good day, I can persuade myself that I am someone who has managed to make a living out of meaning, out of giving words to meaning and meaning to words. But it doesn't always feel that way. When my twelve-year-old son can describe my job, in all sincerity, as 'university meeting arranger', something has surely gone wrong; this is not the free, unfettered life of the mind as I had envisaged it. We are all more or less managing.

Adjusting our expectations is one of the great life skills. This doesn't mean scaling them down or accepting defeat, but it does mean recalibrating our sense of who we (now) are. The brackets dig their claws in: who we *now* are can only be measured against who we used to be. We live our lives cumulatively. My sense of purpose as a child in the 1980s, which according to my boyhood diaries mostly seemed to involve playing football and watching terrible action movies, is not my sense of purpose as an adult in the 2020s, not least because my life has developed into an ever-evolving *search* for purpose. Remembering our past, if we reflect on it as writers and artists continually do, provides a kaleidoscope for remembering our present, an ever-changing light in which to peer at our murky, mundane, magnificent existence. 'You shall never have seen it just this way', in the words of the American poet John Ashbery, 'and that is to be your one reward.' The adjectives alter as the kaleidoscope spins.

'Who we now *are can only be measured against who we used to be.'*

We turn to the past, to put it differently, not just for factual record but for fictional succour. Literature, after all, has a curious metaphysical status: the words on a page are both dead and alive. Fixed for eternity, they are only free once we read them and reimagine them. Their afterlife, to use a term currently fashionable in literary studies, can only take hold in our heads; without a host – without a reader – words are mere zombies, trapped inside their paper tombs. They come to life, however, as soon as they find a brain to feed on. 'A good Booke', in the words of Milton, 'is the pretious life-blood of a master spirit, imbalm'd and treasur'd up on purpose to a life beyond life.' Seen from the perspective of a good book, the present is so much posterity, a time capsule for the purposes of the past.

> *'A good Booke is the pretious life-blood*
> *of a master spirit.'*
> JOHN MILTON

This is all the more so when that past is painful – as all pasts are, sooner or later – since it then imposes a moral imperative on posterity to come to terms with it, to reimagine it as an ongoing source of meaning even now. The Germans, among the most successful recent examples of nations that have faced up to their historical responsibility, have a wonderful term for this: *Vergangenheitsbewältigung*, the process of coming to terms with the past. In some ways the term is misleading, since what is really being addressed is not the past but the present, or rather the continuation of the past *within* the present. The accent, in the end, is on the second half of the noun ('coming to terms with') rather than the first ('the past'), since this is the only part that we can now affect. Literature, as internationally lauded German writers such as Günter Grass and W.G. Sebald have shown us, is an ideal medium for doing this, predicated as it is on the presumption of narrative continuity.

Coming to terms with the past does not, however, mean accepting it. Often it means quite the opposite, criticising the past from the vantage point of the present. Nietzsche, in one of his early essays of the 1870s, identified three modes of history: monumental, antiquarian and critical. Modern Germany had just been founded in 1871, following victory in the Franco-Prussian war, so Nietszche was writing in response to a fever pitch of German nationalism. Yet his argument for the latter, 'critical' mode has lost none of its pertinence in our post-imperial era. Should we accept the monuments of the past, the statues of racists and slavers? Should Rhodes fall? The advantage of taking a critical view of the past, whatever one's views on colonialism and cancel culture, is that it asserts the autonomy of the present, the right of the living to revise or reject the views of the dead. It is not much good, after all, if the tyranny of now simply becomes the tyranny of then.

This is a particular danger given the historical prestige of the humanities. Ever since the Renaissance, Greek and Latin literature have set the standard for Western culture. Historically speaking, there has been more risk of antiquity bias than of recency bias. The early modern period, in particular, was especially beholden to the cachet of the classics, to the idea that legitimacy was automatically conferred through reference to Plato or Sophocles. The philologist, not the poet, became the unacknowledged legislator of meaning. Classical culture came to rival the Bible as the arbiter of authority; the idea of the 'canon', tellingly, began referring not just to religious, but also to classical texts. Authority was bestowed upon ancient authors.

The problem, of course, was that it took its prejudices with it. 'Tradition' handed down not just ideas, but ideology – the chief tenet of which was the superiority of white, Western, educated Man. Writing in the seventeenth century, for instance, the Dutch jurist Hugo Grotius plausibly claimed that 'when many Men of different Times and Places unanimously affirm the same Thing for Truth, this ought to be ascribed to a general Cause' – which seems like a reasonable, consensual statement, until we remember that such consensus was unanimously male. It is hard to escape the fact that responsibility for the 'culture wars', for the embattled identity politics of the twenty-first century, lies to a significant extent with conservative interpretations of the canon, with what one might term 'traditional' approaches to tradition. Minority representation has taken a long time coming: while the classics have long since lost their dominant position, we are only just starting to explore alternative, more inclusive visions of the human condition. 'History is the lie commonly agreed upon', in the much-cited words of Voltaire. Well, we don't agree any more.

The vestigial prestige of the humanities is in many ways

its own worst enemy, since 'high' culture is too easily pitted against 'low' experience – against the historical reality of life as a woman, as a colonial subject, or simply as non-Western. Cultural capital, like its financial counterpart, accrues inexorably to the winner: the 1 per cent unwittingly – or wittingly? – excludes the rest. Questioning this capital, redistributing our emotional investments elsewhere, is indispensable. No one has a monopoly on the past, least of all those of us who continue to draw on its compound interest.

> *'Self-awareness is not in itself sufficient*
> *to save us from history.'*

Can we compound *dis*interest? Nietzsche's critical approach to history suggests one way of doing so, since it takes issue not just with the past but with our ability to interpret the past in any objective manner. The truth is, though, that my own engagement with Nietzsche is itself complicit in all sorts of privileges: in the leisure to read him, the space to expound him, the confidence to cite him. All those seminars and study groups, footnotes and further references, simply reaffirm in the end the existing structures of knowledge and power. Even this acknowledgement, exculpatory as it may seem, is part of the problem, a further twist of the screw that changes nothing. Self-awareness is not in itself sufficient to save us from history.

Perhaps the most honest perspective, however partial it must be, remains the personal rather than the professorial. The anecdote is the antidote, to too much meaning as to too little. I can try to learn from *the* past, but first I must learn from *my* past, from the many minor moments that constitute my brief, irretrievably arbitrary existence. I can learn from Nietzsche, but I should also remember how and when I read Nietzsche, and why he stuck in my head rather than in yours. The misspent truth of my life – too much reading, not enough living – may not be the same as yours or anyone else's, but what we all share is subjectivity, the sense that we are compromised by the same all too human failings of bias and self-regard. I can perhaps escape the tyranny of now; I cannot escape the tyranny of me. The best I can do is come to terms with it.

The lesson for life as we live it now is clear: we must draw on history while keeping a wary distance from it. Learn from the past, to invert Schiller's advice, but do not be its creature; even as we acknowledge the hold that past forms of imagination have on our present-day minds, we must not be beholden to previous ways of doing things or of dreaming them – not least since they might very easily have been otherwise. But nor, of course, should we assume that the latest versions of ideas or arguments are automatically the best. Human life, like human progress, is not Whiggish but zig-zaggish; it does not develop in straight lines, like the Whig view of history, but in stops and starts, like our own view of our life story. In our lives we feel this intuitively, with every step forward accompanied by two steps backwards. In our telling of history, however – and even more so in our telling of technologically driven histories, such as those of science or medicine – we assume that the new supersedes the old.

The advantage of the arts is that this is palpably not the case. Shakespeare is not superseded by Woolf (even if he may be rewritten by her); Chaucer is not undone by Rushdie. Eliot's 'simultaneous order' captures the chronology while overstating it: it is precisely the *non*-simultaneity of past and present that makes them so valuable to each other, since difference is more instructive than sameness. We experience the shock of inequality when we read pro-slavery statements in Horace or Homer, revulsion when we encounter overtly racist statements in Hegel or Kant. Yet such things teach us not so much how far we have come – complacency is odious, as well as demonstrably unjustified – as how different are our laws and lifestyles. The correct conclusion is not to read such figures less, but to read them more, and more critically. The call is not for less past, but for more.

In a very real sense, however, this is one thing that literature rarely provides. Of the 117 billion people who have ever lived, we have records of only a vanishingly small fraction. Books, like battles, are written by the victors, or at least by the survivors. In a commercial sense, too, we gain a false impression of, say, the nineteenth century if we only read the major Realist novels, outsold as they were by sentimental tearjerkers or penny dreadfuls. Literary history, as we understand it in its received, canonical form, is merely the tip of an iceberg in the ocean of time.

That this is true, too, of our own lives – the kaleidoscope of memory captures only the merest fragments of the past, those generic images of playing football that likely populate any boy's memory of the 1980s – suggests one of the great lessons of literature, which is that our minds are shaped not just by everything we have remembered, but by everything we have *forgotten*. Seen from this perspective, *In Search of Lost Time*, surely the single most sustained reflection on this process, constitutes what the great German critic Walter Benjamin termed a 'Penelope-work of forgetting', with every night undoing what the day puts back together. To read and to write – to think – is to do, to undo, and to re-do the stitching of time.

Cultivating Eliot's historical sense means not only remembering, then, but also realising just how much we forget. It is easy to situate ourselves in the lineage of success and prestige; much harder to recover alternative, less flattering perspectives on our own cultural and intellectual development. What we learn from the past depends on where we look – in the pre-prepared places, or in the under-explored byways of cultural history. There is more to be learned by resisting what we know than by reinforcing it, by challenging our preconceptions rather than by cherishing them. This means, among other things, looking beyond received ideas of 'greatness'. We are not just standing on the shoulders of giants, to recycle Bernard of Chartres' time-honoured aphorism, but on those

Figure 6: Little and large: Nicolas Poussin,
Orion aveugle cherchant le soleil (1658)

of Lilliputians, too. We must learn from minor as well as from major literature. The past is not merely Proustian.

In the end, though, the question of aesthetic value remains inescapable. Why do some books attract enduring interest when others don't? Why are some (a few) works read, while many (most) works wither? Context matters, but so too does text: good writing will always remain fresh and interesting. Books of the past command our attention not through their ultimately limited sociological relevance, but through their enduring ability to provoke and stimulate readers. The best writing does this the best ways. Works of merely 'historical' interest are no longer living; in order to speak to us now, the literature of the past must be both of its time and ours, both dated and deathless. Like Baudelaire's famous definition of modernity, it must combine 'the ephemeral, the fugitive, the contingent' with 'the eternal and the immutable'. Finite creatures with infinite thoughts, we require both physics and metaphysics, both history and art. Even in the present, we are always also absent.

Conceived as such, literature teaches us one of the great life skills: how to discriminate. How do we recognise 'the new (the really new)' if we don't know the old? How can we appreciate the living if we don't acknowledge the dead? Taste is no doubt predetermined, to whatever extent, by our upbringing and background, but it is also determined by our curiosity and thirst for knowledge. The more we read, the more we learn not just what we like, but what we *don't* like. *Not* liking is as valid a response to culture as liking, if only we have the confidence to say so. But we can only achieve such confidence through cultivation, through Eliot's 'great labour'. It is emerging as one of the recurring lessons of these ten essays: we can only become autonomous through the example of others.

Learning from the past helps us to reckon with the present. But it also teaches us to unwrap the present, to look inside it and be sceptical of its claims to novelty and pre-eminence. Plenty of people have tried to find the meaning of life before us; plenty have tried to be purposeful. They all died trying. Replacing the tyranny of now with the democracy of the dead is one way to remind ourselves of this basic truth: we later civilisations – as Paul Valéry wrote after the First World War, and as human history has recorded after every war – we too know that we are mortal.

VII

Shape the future

Lesson seven: Things can be different

IF WE LEARN from looking backwards, we live by looking forwards. The invention of the future tense, wrote the critic George Steiner, is one of the supreme mysteries of mankind; it is one of our defining characteristics, our point of difference from hand-to-mouth animals, who can only see a season ahead at best. Our work, our relationships, our children, are all contingent on a conception of futurity, on the assumption that our existence extends beyond the fleeting, fugitive moment. We conclude from past experience that the present will give way to the future.

The eighteenth-century philosopher David Hume famously argued that induction, as this process of inference is known, can provide no logical grounds for the future. On the basis of reason alone, Hume claimed, it is no less implausible to suppose that the sun will *not* rise tomorrow than that it *will*, since 'all arguments concerning existence are founded on the relation of cause and effect; [since] our knowledge of that relation is derived entirely from experience; and [since] all our experimental conclusions proceed upon the supposition that the future will be conformable to the past'. Arguments about the future, in other words, are arguments derived from experience, not from reason – and yet by definition, we have not experienced the future. It may yet be different.

It would be impossible, in any practical sense, to live according to Hume's logic. When I walk to work, I do not doubt that I will get there, since I have taken that same path many times; when I steer my car away from oncoming traffic, I do not doubt that the steering wheel will save me. The sun, to paraphrase Hemingway, also rises. Induction is the basis for all conclusions from cause to effect, and it is the basis, because it has to be, for all assumptions about the future. But induction is not the only way of conceiving what is to come. We also have imagination.

Imagination effectively reverses the laws of induction. What if things were not the same, but different? How would the future look if the sun did *not* rise? Climate change is forcing us to conceive such a scenario quite literally: as human causes increasingly produce inhuman effects, unforeseen catastrophes like Covid are likely to become regular occurrences. Yet our Amazon aesthetics, conversely, leave little room for the unanticipated, imposing a tyranny of induction through their algorithms and pre-determined 'other things we think you might like'. If you enjoyed that product, you'll also enjoy this product: what space remains for difference? In a world that oscillates between the unpredictable and the all too predictable, it is more important than ever that induction be supplemented by imagination.

In the era of the Anthropocene, in the age of the automaton, we will have to imagine new ways of conceiving of ourselves, and new ways of conceiving of the future. Induction is to the understanding as fossil fuel is to climate change: more of the same. What we need is a different kind of conceptual fuel – which is where art comes in. Projecting ourselves into hitherto unsuspected versions of ourselves, into a world untrammelled by cause and effect, is the very essence of the aesthetic. 'Not being able to be in the subjunctive is a big problem for ecological thinking', in the words of Timothy Morton, the so-called philosopher-prophet of the Anthropocene. But it is not a problem for art, since exploring the subjunctive mood – the ability to think counterfactually, to conceive alternative scenarios – is precisely what the imagination does. In everyday speech, we often gloss over the grammar, confusing tenses as we go: if only it was sunnier, we say, when in fact we mean if only it *were* sunnier. Yet the difference is existential, since it is the shift into the subjunctive that characterises the human genius. How *might* things look, what *could* we do? The condition of creativity is the conditional tense.

It is also, however, what we might term the *un*conditional tense. Art opens up a realm untethered to contingency. The brute fact of my bodily existence as I sit in a chair reading a book, or as I stand in a museum looking at a painting, melts away for the duration of my enchantment. It is not that *we* are unaware of our bodies, but that the work of art is, meaning that it does not depend on any single consciousness – even, once it is out in the world, that of its creator. I bring one set of preoccupations to the experience, you bring another: art is like a Rorschach test for reality. We all see different patterns in the inkblot.

This is why the possible meanings of a work of art are never exhausted. Meaning proliferates with every new perspective, as dots on the page become thoughts in the brain. Through the magic of the imagination, through a mere succession of black marks on white paper, we feel our way into the future. Art, in the words of Morton, is 'a sort of gate through which you can glimpse the unconditioned futurality that is a possible condition for predictable futures' – which is artspeak for the idea that imagination creates the future in the process of imagining it, in a kind of infinite feedback loop. They say that in a democracy, we have the governments we deserve. Perhaps the same is also true of the future.

> *'Through the magic of the imagination we feel our way into the future.'*

What can we do to deserve a better future? How can literature help us shape it? Encouraging us to conceive better ways of living, if only implicitly, is surely the true test of any form of art; if it can't do this, there is little point to it. If art is more than a pastime, it is because it does more than merely pass time. However indirectly – and it is often *very* indirectly – art provides us with a moral and metaphysical framework within which to live, a way of conceiving of our lives as something other than simple sustenance. We read and write because we hope to effect some change, however infinitesimally, in our way of seeing the world, our way of being in the world. We read and write because we are invested, however hopelessly, in the idea that things might get better. Like Mandelstam's message in a bottle, even the literature of the past is oriented towards the future.

What we can do to deserve a better future, then, is to imagine it in the first place. We give the literature of the future the name 'science fiction', but really *all* fiction – all writing – is invested in the future, since all writing envisages having an effect on the reader in some way. 'Eco-fiction' has recently become its own sub-genre, but the prefix signals a difference of degree rather than kind. All created things imply their own extension in time and space, their own continuing. The two senses of culture – agriculture and artistic culture – come full circle in explicit renderings of 'ecological' concerns, but they are implicit in any complete vision of the good life. We must cultivate our gardens both literally and metaphorically.

But what do I, what do you, even want from the future? That the question is surprisingly difficult to answer suggests one possible line of response. Many of us, as we sit in the latest pointless meeting with truculent colleagues, as we spend the latest year commuting to an unfulfilling job, would like more space to contemplate an alternative future – which is to say, more space for creativity. There is nothing wrong with the life managerial, but nor is it unreasonable to want to do more with our lives than just manage. What does success look like? A bigger house, a prettier partner, summer in the South of France? Or does it equate to a finer-grained appreciation of the question itself, to the attempt – always elusive, never achieved – to articulate the search for meaning as its own kind of meaning? Can we imagine our way not just into a better future, but into a better *idea* of the future?

The problem with the future is that we can't step back from it, only *into* it. Looking back on my past, it is more or less possible to see myself from the outside, as a different person with different motivations and commitments (we are often embarrassed by our former selves, since we no longer feel that we are the same person). It is also possible, with sufficient training and discipline, to see myself from the outside in the present, to appraise my thoughts and actions as coolly as I might appraise those of someone else – a divestment of self that provides the basis of much philosophy, psychology and religion. But how do we do this with our future? How do we tell anecdotes and marshal evidence about something that has not yet happened?

It is far from certain, after all, that the future will even happen, at least in any recognisably human-centred form. To cite the closing peroration of Michel Foucault's *The Order of Things* (1966), man is a recent invention, soon to disappear 'like a face drawn in sand at the edge of the sea'. The icecaps are melting, the oceans are rising, and our faces are edging ever closer to oblivion. It is against this threat, this constant sense of encroaching loss, that literature can help us stand our ground, not just ecologically but metaphysically. Another modern French writer, contemporary to Foucault, captures this aim of art as well as anyone, describing his desire 'to write, to try meticulously to retain something, to help something survive: to snatch a few scraps from the void that keeps deepening, to leave, somewhere, a furrow, a trace, a mark or some signs'. Georges Perec's shuffling infinitives gesture mournfully towards the receding horizon of the future, as they must, since the shifting sands of the present continuously undermine our attempts to reach it. For the point, of course, is that we *never* reach the future. Once we get there, tomorrow becomes today.

Literature, to pursue Perec's line of thought, is surpassingly good at capturing the way that the future hovers just out of reach. If human consciousness is driven by the tension between tenses – we live physically in the present, but metaphysically in the past and future, in the subjunctive and conditional – then the attempt to reconcile this tension is the fuel that powers the imagination. Proust's search for lost time is merely the most obvious example of the way that we produce literature to forestall finitude. The aim of the game is not so much to pass the parcel as to pass the present: how can we 'snatch a few scraps from the void'? How can we stop the future from hurtling past us?

The answer, of course, is that we cannot. But nor should we want to: the fact that things *can* be different, to take the agenda of lesson seven literally, is the very essence of the future, since without the possibility of difference there *is* no future. To shape the future is not to know it and control it – on the contrary, it is to create space for the emergence of new experiences. This does not, of course, mean that the possibilities are limitless. That the future is a necessarily finite space for each of us as individuals, if not for the species as a whole, is one of the counterintuitive teachings of art. A thing of beauty is *not* a joy for ever, at least not for me or you. The more we accept this, the more we can contribute to the future that transcends us all.

Shaping the future, to put it differently, is actually shaping the present. Art helps us restate the existentially obvious: while I may be thinking about next week, or next year or next century, I am thinking about it *now*. I cannot think in the future (or indeed the past) tense. This, in so many words, is the lesson of one of the major works of world literature, Goethe's *Faust* (1808). Marooned in his study, the desiccated old scholar yearns to be young again, to live a fuller, faster, freer life. Above all, he longs to escape his head, to experience the erotic and physical pleasures of the body: *Faust* is a cautionary tale about the perils of 'pure' thought, the folly of not enjoying life while you can. But it also cautions against wanting to bend the future to your will, against the temptations of time travel. Even if you *could* move backwards and forwards through time with the help of Mephistophelean magic, should you want to? Mephistopheles' great cunning lies in framing the terms of his wager with Faust as a bet against finitude, inveigling Faust into giving up his soul 'if ever to the passing moment I shall say: Beautiful moment, do not pass away!' For to do so, of course, would mean death.

'Art offers us what life cannot: the arc of the imagination.'

Goethe's artful solution is for Faust to have his fate and beat it. After travelling extensively through an alternative universe of classical and mythological heroes, Faust does, finally, utter the fateful phrase – but only, crucially, in the conditional. 'I'd like to gaze on such a land, / On a free earth with free people I'd stand. Then to the moment I'd dare say: Beautiful moment, do not pass away!' The grammar changes everything, as it so often does. Faust *would* utter the words, if only the human condition were otherwise, but he does *not* actually say it in the present indicative. Goethe is thus justified, syntactically speaking, in saving his hero. Unlike in Marlowe's version of the play, although Faust is initially taken away by the diabolical lemurs, he is ultimately redeemed by the 'eternal feminine'. Art offers us what life cannot: the ark of the imagination. The subjunctive saves us.

'We don't just want to be *happy, we want to* become *it.'*

What would any of us dare say to the passing moment? Pass by, is surely the sane answer; it is not, nor should it be, within our gift to stop time. The freeze frame of art can feign such stasis, but there is something uncanny, even necrophiliac, about its tricks and techniques. As Roland Barthes famously noted, photographs are indices of death: the ephemerality of all experience is pinned down like a butterfly, and equally dead. Unlike photography or painting, literature has the advantage that it unfurls over time, at least within the confines of the book. As in life, so in literature we do not take in everything at once – we are obliged to read on. Drawing us on in this manner is the great secret of narrative, an aesthetic response to our existential wiring. For it is the human condition never to be fully satisfied; we are constantly striving, to use the great Faustian verb, towards a better ending, a better future. Our sense of purpose pulls us forward.

This means that the lesson of commandment one recurs, with a change of tense, in the lesson of commandment seven: we don't just want to *be* happy, we want to *become* it. This is why looking forward to something is often more pleasurable than the thing itself, since anticipation of the future is its own source of pleasure. Looking *forward* functions as a self-fulfilling prophecy. To have a conscious purpose, to deliberate deliberately – on what you are going to do next week, next month, next year – is to self-soothe, to administer dopamine to the mind. We might fear the future, we might dread tomorrow, but as long as we have a plan, an agenda of activities, a laundry list for life, we are exerting agency over uncertainty. The illusion of control can itself become a kind of control.

> *'We must imagine the striver, just like we*
> *must imagine Sisyphus, as happy.'*

Imaginative rather than inductive forms of thinking help shape this sense of future-oriented purpose, since they help us conceive of it in the first place. They also show us the importance of *having* a sense of purpose: once Faust stops striving, he dies. A *Streber* in German is a geek, a teacher's pet, someone who is always trying their hardest; but it is also a striver in the metaphysical meaning of the term, someone who is perpetually pushing his rock back up the hill. This is not just a punishment, we must remember. It is also a purpose, an image of a present constantly oriented towards a potential future, albeit one that never comes. We must imagine the striver, just like we must imagine Sisyphus, as happy.

Alongside Faust and Sisyphus, literature offers us one further timeless figure of the striver: Odysseus. The very archetype of the seeker, his odyssey around the Mediterranean continues for some nine years, against almost all the gods. Epic journeys ever since have borne his name – and what is more epic than the journey through time? Odysseus is attempting to return to the home of his past, but where he really arrives, after nineteen years away, is in the house of the future. It is all the more striking, then, that his afterlife – both in the sense of subsequent versions of him and in the sense of his character once he has returned and retired – should place such emphasis on his enduring sense of purpose. Perhaps the most influential version of this occurs in canto 26 of Dante's *Inferno* (c. 1308), where the poet meets the famed voyager in the underworld and hears him recount his final exhortation to his crew as they round the gates of Hercules into unknown waters: 'Consider well the seed that gave you birth: / you were not made to live your lives as brutes, / but to be followers of worth and knowledge.' We are made, Odysseus tells his men, to pursue meaning and illumination; we are made to pursue purpose.

The irony of summoning such wisdom while banished to the underworld, of evoking birth while embracing death, was not lost on Primo Levi, who bitterly recalled these lines among the horrors of Auschwitz. Coining his title *If this is a Man* (1947) in response to the Dantean imperative to 'consider', Levi's opening poem encourages us paradoxically to imagine the truth. 'Consider if this is a man': Levi reminds us, through the echo of Dante, that in Auschwitz they *are* living their lives as brutes. From Homer to hell, across the millennia Odysseus has functioned as the very archetype of human imagination in extreme circumstances.

Many centuries later, Tennyson drew on the same image of the aged Ulysses – to give him his Latin name – in his celebrated poem of 1833:

> Come, my friends,
> 'Tis not too late to seek a newer world.
> Push off, and sitting well in order smite
> The sounding furrows; for my purpose holds
> To sail beyond the sunset, and the baths
> Of all the western stars, until I die.
> It may be that the gulfs will wash us down;
> It may be we shall touch the Happy Isles,
> And see the great Achilles, whom we knew.
> Though much is taken, much abides; and though
> We are not now that strength which in old days
> Moved earth and heaven, that which we are, we are,
> One equal temper of heroic hearts,
> Made weak by time and fate, but strong in will
> To strive, to seek, to find, and not to yield.

Speaking to his crew just as in Dante's poem, Ulysses enjoins them, even in old age and death, to look hopefully to the future. His 'purpose' holds: to sail beyond the sunset. Until the very last he remains a striver, as his famous final infinitives declare, turned towards the future even as the waters wash over him. The poem emphatically makes the point – at the micro level through the repeated subjunctives 'it may be', at the macro level through the very fact of its existence – that the

Figure 7: Striving off into the sunset: Samuel Palmer,
Calypso's Island, Departure of Ulysses, or Farewell to Calypso (1848–9)

imagination takes us places beyond the realms of induction, to 'a newer world'. Ulysses' sailing beyond the sunset, indeed, seems almost to rewrite Hume's sallies about the sunrise, as though new temporal zones required new ways of thinking. It may be that art, Tennyson seems to be saying, can help us find the future.

Which of us isn't looking for it? Like millions of other parents, I can't look at my children without wondering what kind of world we are creating for them. Even the most reactionary of twenty-first-century citizens must acknowledge, to whatever extent, the need to do things differently: climate change and Covid brook no demurral. We cannot wish away our problems. What we can do, however, is frame them in alternative terms, fashion alternative approaches to the basic questions of how and why we are here. Since definitive answers are impossible, we are dependent on the infinitive to provide such suggestions as we can muster: to strive, to seek, to find, and not to yield. The factual world requires the counterfactual word, its imaginative power, its conditionals and subjunctives. In the words of the philosopher Henri Bergson, 'the idea of the future, pregnant with an infinity of possibilities, is more fruitful than the future itself'. Without this idea, without the imagination, we are not fulfilling our purpose.

VIII

Question authority?

*Lesson eight: Speak truth to power –
but speak it slant*

Towards the end of adolescence, in the dog days of the 1990s, I went through a period when I felt that the only adequate response to others was to avoid them. Horrified by the inanity of my peers, repelled by the vanity of my contemporaries, I withdrew to my bedroom and took refuge in great big clouds of marijuana and self-regard. My emerging interest in art and thought, in literature and the life of the mind, required secluding myself from worldly concerns, or so I convinced myself – as though reading precluded living, as though poetry would be contaminated by people. Merely existing – getting up too early, going to bed too late, interacting with my equally confused fellow students – was somehow beneath me. Several years went by this way, in a furious, fatuous, futile haze of stoned self-obsession. I was stuck inside myself.

The Greeks had a technical term for such people: idiots. In ancient Athens, an *idiótēs* (ἰδιώτης) was someone who did not participate in the public sphere, a private, plebeian self. To be apart from the *polis*, to not be engaged in political debate, was to forgo one's responsibilities – and thus one's fully enfranchised status – as an Athenian citizen. Used among others by Herodotus and Plato, as well as over a hundred times in the New Testament, the term *idios* indicates that which is one's own, and thus private; the idiot, by extension, never reaches beyond such privacy to the public sphere. The idiot is stuck inside him- or herself.

Now more than ever, the idiot is the person who thinks that genuine privacy is even possible. Surveillance capitalism has rendered every last aspect of our lives sinisterly accessible; in a sense undreamed of when the slogan first emerged in the 1960s, the personal is the political. With every click and like, every hasty email or instant transfer, we are always already in the public sphere, already plugged into the gathering cloud of human society. For better or worse, wittingly or unwittingly, we are what we share.

We shouldn't think, however, that any of this is new. Change the metaphors, and human interaction has always been imagined as a confederacy of dunces. The 'idiot' becomes intelligent through participation in a larger body. Thomas Hobbes's *Leviathan* (1651), one of the most influential of all works of early modernity, makes the point emblematically through its iconic title page, with the body of the towering Sovereign composed, on closer inspection, out of all the citizens whom he represents. Writing against the backdrop of the English Civil War, Hobbes renders the time-honoured

Figure 8: The body politic: Thomas Hobbes,
Frontispiece to *Leviathan* (1651)

corporeal metaphor literal. The Sovereign, he suggests – the image is irresistible – is the head of a body politic. Both frontispiece and biblical title remain, however, *images*, persuading us through rhetoric as much as through reason. Sovereignty, in Hobbes's argument, is a necessary fiction.

Fiction, conversely, can help us to be sovereign. From Aristophanes to Orwell, from comedy to tragedy, literature has long functioned as a way of speaking truth to power. Reading and writing offer modes of political engagement not just on account of their allegorical plotlines or representative characters – *Animal Farm* as a reckoning with communism, *1984* as an anticipation of the police state – but also owing to their sheer bloody-mindedness. The act of reading, of picking up a book and sitting down quietly, of shutting out the clamorous world for a blessed moment of solitude, is itself an act of autonomy, of self-assertion against what the French thinker Guy Debord called the 'society of the spectacle'. To read is to resist, to assert one's existence as an independent intellectual agent. Private thought can be a public act.

The paradox is that this most solitary of acts binds us to others. The more we cultivate our independence, the more we contribute to the formation of a mature model of interdependence. Even the most self-involved of writers – Pascal with his *Pensées*, Marcus Aurelius with his *Meditations* – encourage us to reflect on our moral presuppositions, which in turn encourages us to reflect on how we relate to others. It is not just the more obvious political allegories, such as those produced after the war by French Existentialists like Sartre or Beauvoir, that are *engagé*. All literature encourages engagement, however indirectly, with the world around us. It does not necessarily make us better people or give us better answers, but it does help us ask better questions. Aesthetic education – reading, writing, reflecting – leads to ethical conclusions.

'The celebration of beauty is a political act.'

It took me a bafflingly long time to realise this. Idiotic adolescent, I persuaded myself that the life of the mind was somehow above the fray of petty politics, a timeless sphere unsullied by mere temporal concerns. Art, I told myself, was the anti-politics – when in fact it is the very essence of politics, if we understand the term not in the narrow sense of parties and governance, but in the broader (and far more interesting) sense of how we engage with the world outside us. Even the most defiantly apolitical of artistic agendas is, for this very reason, profoundly political; to withdraw from the world is to make a statement about it. To return to Wittgenstein's notion of language, there is no such thing as a private literature, since even the poem sitting in a drawer implies a position on the world. The celebration of beauty is a political act.

Growing older, settling into the centre of life, helps us see this. By the time we have reached our forties we are involved in so many overlapping constituencies – workplaces, schools, families, running groups – that idiocy is no longer an option. Authority accrues through the mere passage of time, as we move from the margins of power to the middle. Our inner adolescent wants to stay cool and cynical, but our outer adult recognises the need to pay bills and take decisions, however difficult they may be. We can dress down as much as we like, we can continue to wear the scuffed Converse and faded T-shirts of our youth, but we still have to take responsibility for children and choices. We have to *answer* for authority as much as question it.

Perhaps this is why I transferred my allegiance from music to literature as I emerged from adolescence. Independent music became interdependent literature: words, and the vast history of all those who had used them so eloquently before me, became a way of accepting life rather than rebelling against it. It is not that my rebellious streak disappeared, but that it became part of a subtler set of questions about how to revise life rather than reject it. Sold on subtlety – the very pronunciation of which, I always felt, suggests its depths, the silent 'b' of hidden meaning – I developed a preference for oblique, abstract writing, for adult art over teenage angst. Questioning authority began taking on a different form.

'We have to answer *for authority*
as much as question it.'

The political commitments of literature are not limited to the more strident strains of didacticism pursued by the likes of Orwell, Sartre or Brecht (or by their counterparts on the right wing, such as Pound or Céline). In literature as in life, obliquity is often a more productive strategy than confrontation, since it allows us to develop political positions without overtly insisting that this is what we are doing. 'Tell all the truth but tell it slant', in the memorable words of Emily Dickinson – which is another way of saying: show, don't tell. *Speak truth to power but speak it slant* might be a manifesto for the politics of literature.

'Tell all the truth but tell it slant.'
EMILY DICKINSON

Understood in such terms, the slant emerges as a variation on the subjunctive or conditional, as a way of enabling us to see that life *might* be different to how it currently is. The angles of existence do not all point straight ahead: we can cut corners, and see around them, with the help of (other people's) imagination. Perhaps the most powerful variation on the idea that the slant of writing implies a kind of politics is the Romanian poet Paul Celan's notion of the 'meridian'. As developed in a speech of 1960, Celan's term suggests that poetry serves as a marker of both distance and proximity: the meridian of language connects us to others while at the same time measuring – and protecting – our essential privacy. A German-speaking survivor of the Holocaust, Celan's relationship to the world was nothing if not ambiguous: his parents, after all, were murdered in the language in which he wrote. His poetry, most famously the emblematic poem 'Death Fugue', in which the sombre music of his cadences mimics the *danse macabre* of the death camps, is both profoundly private and searingly public. The personal, in Celan's case, was all too political.

All of us must measure our position on the meridian of language. Language is our primary mode of interaction with others; as such, its accurate and imaginative usage matters a great deal. As John Milton writes in *Areopagitica* (1644), perhaps the single most important manifesto for free speech in the English language:

> Books are not absolutely dead things but doe contain
> a potencie of life in them to be as active as that soule
> was whose progeny they are; nay they do preserve
> as in violl the purest efficacie and extraction of that
> living intellect that bred them. I know they are as
> lively, and as vigorously productive, as those fabulous
> Dragons teeth; and being sown up and down, may
> chance to spring up armed men.

Written at the height of the Civil War, Milton's plea for promiscuous reading resounds throughout the ages, and indeed throughout this book (I have already alluded to it several times). Be careful with those dragons' teeth, Milton whispers to us. They may spring up armed men.

For the greatest English-language 'political' writer of the twentieth century, it was self-evident that the careful use of words is itself a political act. In his famous essay of 1946, 'Politics and the English Language', George Orwell makes the case for clarity and concision as the guiding principles of public discourse. Crucially, he sees language as both cause and effect: it 'becomes ugly and inaccurate because our thoughts are foolish, but the slovenliness of our language makes it easier to have foolish thoughts'. Good writing helps us retain freshness of thought; bad writing, conversely, deadens our sensibilities. In the post-war period, suggests Orwell, 'the present political chaos is connected with the decay of language', which is why linguistic precision is 'not the exclusive concern of professional writers'. We should all be concerned by cliché.

Even more in the early twenty-first century than when Orwell wrote these words in the mid-twentieth, 'there is no such thing as "keeping out of politics"'. To be fully idiotic in the era of instant communication is no longer possible: language is political, and we all use language. It does not follow, however, that political writing is therefore good writing. As Orwell notes, political writing is in fact often bad writing, at least if it is conceived as a way of expounding predetermined dogma. For dogma rapidly becomes dogmatism, which in turn takes refuge in abstract aims and all-purpose euphemism. The message – to convince the reader of the righteousness of a particular political stance – emasculates the medium. The best writers, conversely, make the medium a part of the message by telling it slant, stimulating our political consciousness in ways that *make us feel* a given position or perspective, rather than simply hammering us over the head with it. Words must affect us if they are to have an effect on us.

This, of course, is why despots and dictators have long feared the power of literature. The slant of art encourages us to question authority, since it encourages us to think – and to feel – for ourselves. As Orwell shows, however, it teaches us to question not just the ruler, but also the writer. 'Authority', in the first instance, accrues to the author: while we are reading a text, we are at the mercy of its movements, however much we may rewrite it in our heads. Roland Barthes's great battle-cry of 1967 announcing the 'death of the author' rebels against this power dynamic, representing nothing so much as an expression of the post-war rejection of social deference. Barthes tells us, quite literally, to question authority. We must not take what we read – or see, or experience – at face value; we must not accept received wisdom just because it is easier. We should discover, rather, the sense of liberation that comes with questioning even the questioners. 'Critical thinking', as developed through studying the humanities, is one of the great transferable thrills.

What happens, though, when the criticism itself becomes a cliché? 'Orwellian' is an overused adjective; 'Kafkaesque' captures totalitarianism to a fault. If achieving adjectival status is a mark of distinction for a writer, it is also a mark of dilution, applying the idiom so broadly as to diminish its original force. Authority attenuates as well as amplifies; as anyone who has ever held a leadership position comes to realise, being reduced to a small set of characteristics, – responsible, representative, reactionary – hardly does justice to the complexity of human character. Whenever we see our teachers (or parents, or bosses) off duty, they seem like different people, not just relaxed but enlarged, freed from the constrictions of command. Such authority as any of us has, as I have in writing this essay, is only ever one aspect of us, the public face of private doubt. George Orwell was also Eric Blair.

It is not just authority that we should question, but the very idea of 'authority'. The question mark in the title of this chapter is as much interrogative as imperative. It points to a subtler problem behind the posturing. Do we want to question *all* authority? Is it really in our interests to undermine it? The slogan has intuitive appeal. Who doesn't like to see themselves as a radical free spirit? But as soon as we think through its consequences it is far from clear that they are universally desirable. In the absence of authority, all structure of meaning becomes impossible: how do we orient our lives and ambitions without some sense of oversight or underwriting? How would we even know when we are winning? 'Authority' is a moving target, evolving over the years as our frame of reference changes. We do not kick against the same pricks at fifty as at fifteen, nor, thankfully, do we feel the same need to. Authority need not be authoritarian, whatever the sixties told us.

Perhaps, then, we should aim to *soften* authority rather than to question it. To soften authority is to acknowledge its necessity while at the same time seeking to blunt its cruder blows. It is to try to be a force for good, but by working *with* a given power structure, rather than against it. Colleagues who cavil constantly are tiresome, since their quibbling means that nothing can ever move forward. The sanest, most pragmatically productive position in any power structure is that of the insider-outsider, what the philosopher Stanley Cavell calls the 'intimate outsider' – someone who steps up while stepping back, who helps push power in the direction of benevolence while maintaining a critical distance from it.

Literature, as leaders such as Barack Obama have long acknowledged, can play a crucial role in refining this position. For literature necessarily adopts the posture of the insider-outsider, seeking a perspective outside our experience in order to gain purchase on it. That there is no Archimedean point from which to do so is the reason why we are all, ultimately, so many people in a Pirandello play, so many characters in search of an author. In a Godless world, we must find – and create – our own authority. Reading widely can help us do this. It can help refine our judgement of when (and when not) to accept a given voice or argument. To make decisions we need to know not just how to read a text, but how to read a room.

Softening authority in this manner is the mature version of adolescent 'questioning', since it acknowledges the inevitable *Realpolitik* of human interaction, the need for compromise and concession. We cannot keep reinventing the real; sometimes we have to accept, or even impose, its hidden strictures. Sometimes we have to short-cut the longitudinal study. Fact-checking, falsifiability and footnotes may be the markers of intellectual authority, but they are not the emblems of emotional integrity. We don't, thank God, apply scientific rigour to our daily routine. There is no bibliography for breakfast, lunch and supper. We do, however, accept the necessity of some such arrangement, just as we accept the necessity of overarching intellectual structures such as 'early modern' or 'English literature', however arbitrary and culturally constructed they may be. The interdisciplinary author still requires disciplinary authority; we don't want breakfast, lunch and supper all at once. Clarity begins at home.

This obvious point that literature creates authority as much as it questions it finds its way into our lived experience. The older we get, the more we become not just questioners but also respondents, responsible for authority. The slant leans both ways, backwards and forwards, inwards and outwards. We must question authority, but only up to a certain point; we must tell it slant, but also say it straight. We can't live exclusively in the interrogative; we also need the subjunctive, and sometimes just the plain old indicative. Orwell notwithstanding, the acceptance of cliché as a currency of meaning, not only at the linguistic level of received idioms but at the conceptual level of received ideas, is a necessary part of public life.

To question *everything*, after all, is to question nothing, since it obviates the hard work of making fine-grained, value-based distinctions. Taken seriously as a philosophical argument it is a dead end, or rather a no-end: to question *all* authority is to question even this question, and then to question the question about the question, and so on in an infinite regress of non-meaning, an anarchy of evasion. We cannot, in the end, live our lives this way; we have to ground our meaning somewhere. It is much better – and much harder – to differentiate between earned and unearned authority, between authentic and inauthentic ways of thinking. It has taken me the twenty years since idiotic adolescence to realise this: not all cliché and commonplace is worthless. Sometimes the plain prose moves us on as well.

'We have to ground our meaning somewhere.'

The purpose of the imagination, then, is to help us not so much to refute the status quo as to refine it. To participate in any act of literature is to step back from life as well as into it, or to step back from life *in order* to step back into it. Every act of the imagination, whether sitting down with a book or poising your fingers over the keyboard, comes at the cost of a hundred other more pressingly political concerns. To live is to choose; to write is to exclude, as well – however select-ively – as to include. What we read or write is inescapably partial, in both senses of the term. With all the pathos of their fateful year of composition, Brecht's lines of 1939, written in

Swedish exile as the Second World War began, hover reproachfully over every writer: 'What times are these, in which / A conversation about trees is almost a crime / For in doing so we maintain our silence about so much wrongdoing!' All literature – all art – that is not directly denunciatory is a conversation about trees, disdaining to address the larger wood.

The escape hatch, however, lies in the 'almost'. If we are to question authority, as agitators everywhere have always encouraged us to do, then we must also question that of Brecht, or at least allow for the sleight of hand with which he undermines his own authority. For his statement is, of course, self-undoing. The conversation about trees is only almost – and so in fact, *not* – criminal on account of its self-consciousness, of the way it reverses into making a broader political statement by not making a broader political statement. Brecht fears maintaining silence, and by articulating this fear he breaks his silence; he fears complicity, and by identifying this fear he denounces complicity. Exiled into idiocy, banished into an imposed privacy outside their native idiom, poets write back but write obliquely. Literature speaks truth to power, but speaks it slant. In the angles of such art we see our own existence, writ large.

IX

Aim high – and miss

Lesson nine: Fail again, fail better

TO COME LAST, to come second, to come not quite first: for most of us, most of the time, this is the human condition. It is also one of contemporary culture's great unwritten topics. We celebrate success and hide failure, but which is the more interesting? From moral victory to abject incompetence, the spectrum of failure is much broader than the palette of success; every winner is alike, to paraphrase Tolstoy, but every unsuccessful venture is unsuccessful in its own way. If poets, in the old Aristotelian argument, are superior to historians because they show us what *might* have been, so too do the runners-up and losers, the counterfactual figureheads of our collective imagination. Literature abounds in such figures. Can we learn from them?

Throughout my childhood, there was always one boy – I didn't notice the girls until later – who was better than I. Better at maths, better at sports, better at everything. Raphael at junior school became William at senior school, but the pattern stayed the same: I was good at some things, better at other things, but never quite best at anything. There was always someone that bit better than I was.

I've often wondered what effect this has had on my life. Was I fated to be one of life's also-rans, in the first rank but not at the very front? Or did this secondary position, tucked in just behind the leader, make me perfectly placed to overtake at the final moment? More to the point, what effect did it have on my developing morality, on my sense of others and my relationship to them? Perhaps being second best really was an instance of that great cliché of English education, 'character-building'. Perhaps not coming first builds our characters all the way into adulthood.

Winning is unequivocal, whether in school or in life. Success brooks no argument. It is the horizon by which we orient our lives, the parameter of possibility behind the 'protestant work ethic' that drove, in Max Weber's famous argument, the triumph of Western capitalism. Failure, on the other hand, is bitterly contested. Its grades and ranks are infinitely subdivisible into a constantly shifting hierarchy of more or less acceptable, more or less shameful concessions. This hierarchy is the mood music of our lives, its many minor accommodations – I never really wanted the job in the first place, I'm better off without her – the precondition of our *amour-propre*. Failure, and our constant negotiation with it, is the shadow side of narcissism.

Which of us doesn't fail on a daily basis? The set-pieces of success are easy to assess: election nights, sports tournaments, appointments, promotions. Far more insidious, because they are far more ubiquitous, are all those everyday attempts at self-improvement: getting fitter, staying calmer, becoming smarter. That we fail at these is built into the process, since unlike elections and tournaments there is no external framework, no finishing line to tell us whether we have, or have not, decisively won. Failure is the precondition for success, not just in the Hallmark sense of glib sentiment ('before every success there is a failure'), but in the broader sense that the one is the measure – and thus also the promise – of the other. We can only get fitter because we are not (yet) fit enough.

Celebrity culture pounds us incessantly with the propaganda of success. The demigods of the gossip pages are avatars of ambition, semi-mythical figures onto whom we project our collective sense of what it means to 'make it'. In our age of the image, much of this is visual, the shiny teeth and glossy hair, the glittering repetitions of desire. If their ephemerality is obvious – tabloid editors, like Ezra Pound, must constantly 'make it new' – so is their inverse. Few pleasures are greater, it would seem, than catching the beautiful off-guard, spotting the cellulite behind the celebrity. The (supposedly) moral failing of being less than perfect is the flipside of fame: *Schadenfreude* is the price of success. Secretly, we want our gods to fail.

Literature is the record of such failure, or rather the record of turning such failure into success. Art is a kind of alchemy, in which the base matter of bitter process becomes the precious material of the achieved product. The sheer fact of recording ephemeral experience, of imagining an alternative way of being beyond our daily grind, raises it out of the flow of time – time, of course, being our biggest and surest failure. The temporal self-consciousness on which all great art is predicated tracks and transcends our mortality, freezing the words that we read or write into so many versions of yesterday's thoughts while at the same time allowing us to travel backwards and forwards across them. The house always wins, but as long as we are in it, we can redecorate.

To put it another way, art encourages us to aim high. The best that has been thought and said: the superlative is built in, however we may now define it. What this means, naturally enough, is that failure is also built in, since in aiming high we will very often miss. But these are the terms on which art encourages us to live, to stretch ourselves on the spectrum from occasional success to recurring failure. A man's reach should exceed his grasp, or what's a heaven for? Serpentining beauty – so Robert Browning's poem about the Renaissance painter Andrea del Sarto teaches us – is not meant to be easy.

*'The house always wins, but as long as
we are in it, we can redecorate.'*

Our relationship to ambition remains, however, a curious thing. We encourage it and deplore it in equal measure. We want people to be ambitious, but we don't want them to be *too* ambitious. No one likes the politician or colleague who too obviously has their eyes on advancement, even though every politician or colleague obviously has their eyes on advancement. Used about a project or proposal, 'ambitious' is often intended as a front-handed insult, condemnation disguised as compliment. Look it up in a thesaurus and the ambiguity jumps out: from 'aspiring' to 'competitive', 'desirous' to 'difficult', the first four letters alone exemplify the ambivalence. I remember once being described as 'forward' in a job interview; I didn't get the position. If ambition is a desirable quality, so too is learning how to hide it.

No one wants to encourage their children to aim low. To urge ambition, though, is also to urge adversity, or at least an acceptance of its inevitability. It is the stuff of a thousand self-help clichés. You have to lose before you can win; success is based on failure; the struggle is its own reward. It would be easy to align a series of inspirational quotations from authors across the ages – failure changes us for the better, success for the worse, to cite the age-old sentiment – but it would also be facile, since such statements simply rewrite failure as a different kind of success. To write honestly is not to hide the struggle or to reconceptualise it as ultimately triumphant; it is to turn its lining inside out to face the world *as failure*.

The patron saint of this reversal is surely Montaigne, who pioneered the essay form as an attempt at self-revelation. Experience, as Montaigne has it in his most emblematic of essays, is the greatest tutor precisely because it is largely a synonym for failure; ageing, if nothing else, assures us of this.

'Perpetual dissatisfaction is the price of ambition, or what's a heaven for?'

Rather than viewing failure as preparation for success, success must be reconceived as failure – or at least, as *insufficient* success – for it to be able to continue. 'No powerful mind stops within itself', writes Montaigne in his final essay 'On Experience': 'it is always stretching out and exceeding its capacities'. Perpetual dissatisfaction is the price of ambition, or what's a heaven for?

The trick is to learn to live with such dissatisfaction. The purpose of art, to put it differently, is simultaneously to satisfy and dissatisfy us. It satisfies us through its surpassing beauty; it dissatisfies us through its contrasting distance from our daily lives – how could we ever achieve *that*? – as well as through the melancholy recognition of its inevitable imperfection. To the Keatsian paradigm of negative capability, and the Kantian oxymoron of purposiveness without purpose, we can add a third paradox: dissatisfied satisfaction. Art, literature, the life of the mind can help give us meaning precisely by withholding meaning, by accepting, even celebrating, the fact that our lives are never fully complete. Dissatisfaction is an essential element of the human condition, the grain of fault in the recipe of existence. Powered by paradox, we always want more.

For what would supreme satisfaction actually mean? At

best it is a religious state, outside our earthly realm of traffic jams and taxes and gossip; or a sexual state, as ephemeral as an orgasm. Nothing fulfils us once and for all, nor should we want it to. To have achieved everything, to hope for nothing, would in the final analysis mean death – or stasis, the Faustian renunciation of further hope. The dissatisfied human condition is to keep moving forwards, or at least to aspire to do so; Odysseus, the founding figure of Western literature, is defined by his journey, not by his destination. In the words of advice given to him by the modern Greek-Egyptian poet Constantine Cavafy: 'Keep Ithaka always in your mind. / Arriving there is what you're destined for. / But don't hurry the journey at all. / Better if it lasts for years'. No matter how hard, how problematic our own odyssey may at times be, the lesson is clear: it is better to struggle than to arrive.

That we can continue to struggle – that we can try again, fail again, and fail better – is what it means to be alive. Samuel Beckett's emblematic imperatives are the opposite, in effect, of Faust's moment of supreme satisfaction. Beautiful moment, do not pass away. Art entices us with access to the infinite – while of course in reality, we remain all too finite. All we can do is fail again, and fail better. For all its moments of great beauty, Beckett's writing is above all a paean to the import-ance of relentlessness, to the sheer doggedness of what the French poet Paul Éluard, writing in 1946, called *le dur désir de durer*. The difficult desire to endure: repetition is raised not just to an art form, but to a way of life. Where lesser writers stumble into tautology (see my echoing awkward 'all' in the sentences above), Beckett sharpens the sentiment to the point of paradox: 'You must go on. I can't go on, I'll go on.' In contrast to the Faustian moment of stasis, going on – *continuing*, in Beckett's original French – is both an admission of failure and a marker of success, the only one that really matters. Who speaks of victory? asks Rilke in one of his great elegies. To endure is all.

The lesson for life, then, is clear: it is not whether we win or lose that defines us, but whether we keep trying. To aim high is first and foremost to *aim*. Even if the arrow misses, it is still in flight, to vary Zeno's paradox. Whatever meaning we give to the phrase 'the project of our life', it is not static or fixed once and for ever. It is really the project*s* of our life, the succession of goals that draw us ever forwards. I for one feel most unsure of myself, most unfocused, whenever I don't have a target to aim at. As long as I have a sense that I am inching forwards, however incrementally – with a book, a project, a friendship – the satisfaction is not *merely* dissatisfied. Without such horizons, all we have is the stasis of Sundays, the slow stagnation of long summer holidays; purposiveness has no purpose.

'Who speaks of victory? asks Rilke.
To endure is all.'

In a sense, I'd even go so far as to say, the nature of the target is irrelevant. What matters is that there *be* one. The nature of purpose, by analogy, is irrelevant; what matters is that we find one. The nihilistic despair that characterises so much post-war thought – what the Existentialists termed the 'absurd' – is only nihilistic if we see life as *mere* endurance, as empty and meaningless. Sisyphus becomes happy, however, if we allow that the transition from stasis to movement, from not being able to go on to going on, is itself a meaningful achievement. Which means that failure is the precondition for life *because*, not although, it is the precondition for further failure. I do not always conform to my own commandments. I am at times as self-centred and sullen, as incapable of joy as the next man. But this does not vitiate the advice. I can't go on, I'll go on.

This self-propelling, open-ended quality of ambition, its inability to settle on any final sense of supreme satisfaction, has a long and distinguished artistic history. In the preface to his *Natural History* (c. AD 77), Pliny the Elder identi-fied the category of works of art signed in the imperfect – as opposed to the perfect – tense: I *was doing* this rather than I *did* this. Such a signature replaces the created implications of the achieved product with the creative implications of the on-going process, since it suggests that the artist may yet return to the painting. He may yet pick it up again. The best-known example of this so-called 'Plinian signature' is that of Titian, for instance in his late *Annunciation*, at the foot of which the visible autograph *Titianus fecit* hides – as

Figure 9: Titian was here:
Titian, *Annunciation* (c. 1564)

studies have shown – the more tentative *Titianus faciebat*. The shift from perfect to imperfect moves the artwork away from something that the artist considered *made* towards something that he was *in the process* of making, and thus with any luck may yet remake. Titian's signature illustrates dissatisfied satisfaction, in other words, in its very etymology. Failure is factional, it is in the very nature of making. But so, potentially, is success.

Artists or not, all our lives, as we live them, are written in the imperfect. As the name suggests, it is the tense of incompletion – the tense not just of failures past but of futures potent, since it keeps open the space for further development. The perfect, after all, is the tense of death, of that which is complete; much better to remain imperfect and incomplete. Much better, if we can only find the courage, to retain the possibility of re-making ourselves.

Literature offers us an image of such possibility. From Aristotle onwards, tragedy in particular has supposedly served a cathartic function, purging us of emotion and regulating our psychic excess. As a genre, of course, it is defined by failure, by the unhappy ending of an unhappy few; yet it is an ersatz failure, an aesthetic scapegoat for our existential woes. The implication of Aristotle's theory of catharsis is that tragedy fails so that we don't have to. Art recasts our negative emotions, through the filter of someone else's failure, into positive energy. Feel again, feel better.

'The pendant to ambition is not, in the end, failure; it is frailty.'

The prerequisite for such cathartic moments, however, is that we acknowledge our need for them in the first place. The pendant to ambition is not, in the end, failure; it is frailty. To aim high is not just to accept that, most of the time, most of us miss, but to accept that we must expose ourselves to shame, humiliation and desire, all the ugly, unflattering emotions that we work so hard to hide from each other. The very idea of 'exposing yourself', with its sniggering connotations of an old man in a mackintosh, suggests the power of the taboo. No one wants to expose themselves; no one wants to lay themselves open to ridicule. Yet this is precisely what we do when we write or paint, when we publish or exhibit: we hang it all out there. It is precisely what we do, or what we should do, when we live: make ourselves vulnerable.

Scholarship trains us in modes of self-suppression. We are taught to pretend that the academic author, like the monarch, is not a subject; we feign objectivity through avoiding the first-person singular, or by couching our claims in the passive. Armed with impersonality, the worst that can happen is that we misunderstand a text, or misrepresent its author's intentions. The stakes of subjectivity are kept deliberately low; emotion, if it happens to intrude, is an interloper from another language game. Pathos is prohibited.

Such strictures may be a distinct advantage for the scientific pursuit of knowledge, but they are not how most of us experience either art or life. We *want* to be moved, to be enticed or entranced, entertained or irritated. We have a palpable design on art, whether or not it has one on us: we want the words to have an impact. Equally, we have a palpable design on life: we want to live it, ideally 'to its fullest'. To do so, though, we have to put ourselves out there, own up to the idea of wanting and needing. The very term 'want' suggests as much: we desire that which we lack.

If I am doubtless revealing my own pathology, it is singularly appropriate to the point I am trying to make. Need, for me, has always been a four-letter word. 'Neediness' was the great bogeyman of my childhood, raised as I was by the wolves of boarding school. It has taken me half a lifetime to see (but will I ever see it?) that to love is to need (but will I ever feel it?), that the armature of self-sufficiency so carefully constructed around the outsourced child excludes, rather than enables, true insight. To live through literature, to feel through the mind, is to this extent a trap. It is a way of constructing a castle around the proud, embattled self – at the bottom of which, as Flaubert memorably remarked, beats a tide of shit. To aim truly high is to open the portcullis and lay down the drawbridge.

No more ivory towers of impersonality, then; no more fragments shored against my ruin. Vulnerability is the very essence of the human condition. To be is to need. My boys, my ideal needers, have taught me this much. Can literature, can the life of the mind, help us see it too? The empathy of the imagination is one thing; the received – and often very gendered – ideas of the tradition, quite another. It is not because the ideal of individual fortitude goes back all the way to the Stoics, to Diogenes in his bathtub asking nothing more of Alexander than that he get out of his sunlight, that the tradition is unproblematic. The rejection of external ephemera that has functioned, over the millennia, as the decisive criterion for true self-sufficiency is also decisively (toxically?) male. For the macho self, neediness is weakness. Empathy, conversely, has always been categorised as recognisably female, which explains the cliché of women as the principal readers of novels. Can re-evaluating what we mean by 'failure' move us beyond such tired stereotypes?

The question, in the end, is whether the literary representation of emotion – as well as the sheer fact *of* representing emotion – can help us to rethink the relationship between ambition and anxiety. What does it mean to fail better? If the phrase is anything more than a pleasing paradox, it must mean not that failure is the precondition for success, but that failure can actually *be* success. It just depends on the terms in which we articulate the idea: as self-reliance or self-knowledge, ability or vulnerability. Our penultimate commandment is not only to aim high in life – who doesn't want this? – but to ask what such aim entails, and what are its consequences and costs. To identify such expenses is to identify what we want from life, and what kind of person we want to be – which is to say, surely, not the most *prestigious* version of ourselves, but the most *purposeful*, the most fully attuned to our own imperfect signature. 'I'm proof against that word failure', states George Eliot's radical Felix Holt. 'I've seen behind it. The only failure a man ought to fear is failure of cleaving to the purpose he sees to be best.' Even if we miss, to aim high is to aim on purpose.

X

Think for yourself

Lesson ten: Forget everything you have read

LITERATURE, it should by now be clear, is a double-edged word. If it can liberate us from previous strictures of thought and feeling, it can also impose new strictures – not least, the misplaced belief that literature *suffices* for a meaningful life, which of course it doesn't. The purpose it provides can be a pitfall; like Alice, the unwary reader risks disappearing down the rabbit-hole of her imagination. Writing is even worse: start drafting a book, and before you know it several years have passed unremarked. The draw of literature is also the drug of literature, the ever-addictive intuition that greater meaning lies just around the corner, just over the next page. 'I don't take drugs, I take books', wrote Ingeborg Bachmann in her sprawling novel *Malina* (1971). Books are made of words, and 'words are, of course, the most powerful drug used by mankind', as Rudyard Kipling told the Royal College of Surgeons in 1923. 'Not only do words infect, egotize, narcotize, and paralyze, but they enter into and colour the minutest cells of the brain.' Reading forms us and informs us. But might it also deform us?

> *'The more we furnish our minds, the more we have to keep an open mind.'*

The first and last lesson of all thought is that we must learn to think for ourselves. Kant's metaphor for Enlightenment applies to us all: to lead the fullest life possible, we must find ways to emerge from our self-incurred immaturity. We must find the courage to use our *own* intellect. Reading widely is the surest path to doing so – to be 'intelligent', etymologically speaking, is to read between things – which is why totalitarian states have always sought to prevent it. But there is danger in outsourcing our thoughts to thinkers more eloquent and powerful than we: namely, that we start to think (too much) like them. The final paradox of literature for life, in other words, is that the more we furnish our minds, the more we have to keep an open mind.

It is a paradox to which professional readers are particularly susceptible. My wife often gets irritated if I refer in the middle of a conversation to an author or text. She views it as a way of not engaging with whatever we are discussing, as yet another English evasion. She is surely right. Literary critics suffer from a kind of professorial Tourette's syndrome, a reflex twitch of reference and allusion always at the edges of our attention. The slightest pretext can summon a pre-text, as thoughts go spinning off like 'threads of connection' (*Middlemarch*). Such threads enrich the fabric of consciousness, no doubt about it, and provide the basis, as this book has shown, for a moral as well as aesthetic apprehension of existence. In truth, though, they are as defensive as they are progressive, a way of warding off final meaning through constant slippage and deferral. '"Like" and "like" and "like"' – my over-developed memory of Virginia Woolf reminds me – 'but what is the thing that lies beneath the semblance of the thing?' Critics suffer, almost inevitably, from allusions of grandeur.

What is the answer? How are we to continue enriching our minds without getting tangled up in all those threads? We might begin by realising, I think, that we are not beholden to the thoughts of others, no matter how eloquent or persuasive they may be. We are not simply the sum total of everything we have ever read; we have our own ideas and our own voices, and we should not be afraid to raise them. No matter how much we educate ourselves, no matter how widely we read, in the end we must ignore the paths of others and steer our own course. In the end, we must learn to think for ourselves.

Throughout this book, I have been trying to do precisely that – and now I am encouraging you, dear reader, to do so in turn. If that means rejecting or disagreeing with my ten 'commandments' and formulating your own set of lessons, so much the better; my work here will have been done. For such is the insight, after reflecting on purpose, that we must finally reach: we should forget everything we have read, or at least we should not fetishise it. How else can we develop as truly autonomous agents? It is no good emancipating ourselves from the peer pressure of life in order simply to bind ourselves to the peer pressure of literature. We must learn, rather, to negotiate – and to renegotiate and renegotiate – our own freedoms, from our predecessors as well as from our contemporaries. We must learn to be free.

'We are not simply the sum total of everything we have ever read'

The problem is, however, that if we are all reading the same books, we will all have the same references. This is a good thing if it encourages a common store of cultural knowledge, but a bad thing if it discourages fresh, original thought. My closest friend has had much of the same education that I have, and many of the same experiences; it means, happily, that each of us knows how the other is likely to think. But it also means, unhappily, that we each know how the other is likely to think. Repetition and pre-programming are the price of education. In many ways, they are its definition. We can't develop our own view on something until we have sifted through the views of others.

When I was in graduate school, I convinced myself in the way that only earnest young graduate students can that

I was cultivating moral and intellectual independence from the society around me. The truth, of course, was that I was cultivating *dependence* – on my teachers and masters, on the writers and thinkers I was eagerly inhaling into my bloodstream. Over time I developed a tolerance, perhaps even an immunity, to their worst excesses, but the habit remained, the critical cringe towards the higher power of the better read. Now that I am in turn one of the better read, I cringe at my credulity. Does anyone really want to be like *me*? I'm barely sure that I do.

The communities that we inhabit define us as much as they develop us. My own evolution in the hothouse of the humanities is a case in point. The environment of a doctoral programme at an elite university breeds certain stock types, ripe for a campus comedy. Here they come now, the central casting of the over-educated: young fogey, stooped and professorial at the age of twenty; critical theorist, hanging on every new pronouncement from Paris; saturnine goth, eyes rimmed with mascara and mystery. Competition brings inflation, a constant pressure to sound smarter, look cooler, talk faster. Identity becomes identical, or at least identifiable, an open future reduced to a pre-packaged present. Everyone is trying hard to impress. No one is really thinking for themselves.

It would be easy to identify similar codes for other subcultures: doctors, soldiers, charity workers. The paradox is particularly striking, though, for a profession supposedly defined by its credo of independent thought: most of us, most of the time, think the same way. This is no doubt natural enough and in itself no bad thing. Consensus is necessary for co-operation. But the question accrues as we continue evolving: how do we retain our own voice? As we grow up, we caricature ourselves into meaning not only because of our natural (and, often, correct) tendency to defer to authority, but because we don't know any better. We are making ourselves up as we go along.

Yet this very realisation should itself be instructive, enabling us as it does to *continue* thinking rather than merely regurgitating pre-digested ideas. Thought emerges as much – if not more – from what we don't yet understand as from what we do. In his brief essay 'On the Gradual Construction of Thoughts during Speech' (1805–6), Heinrich von Kleist suggests that 'if there is something you want to know and cannot discover by meditation, I advise you to discuss it with the first acquaintance whom you happen to meet. He need not have a sharp intellect, nor do I mean that you should question him on the subject. No! Rather you yourself should begin by telling it all to him.' We are waking ourselves up as we go along.

Using others to sharpen our own views is, of course, something we do all the time. Knowing how to take what there is to learn from a situation – from events, from experiences, from people – and then move on to the next thing is an important life skill, however callous it can sometimes seem. There is something Oedipal, to put it in Freudian terms, about all developmental processes. Even if we don't want to kill our teachers, it is natural and often necessary to take our distance from them, if only to continue growing on our own terms. Literature provides a laboratory for such processes, not least because we can move away from certain books or writers and then return to them later, once our perspective on their purposes has changed. Even if we outgrow an author or teacher, they still leave their imprint on our identity.

Equally, however, we would do well to distrust our constructed identities. It is not because we have read a text or imagined an experience that it is necessarily to our benefit; it is not because we have struggled through Proust or Plato that every line they ever wrote is unimprovable, forever to be cited for our edification. People refer to Shakespeare as though he were an ultimate authority, but in reality the precise pitch of his moral force depends on the character who is speaking. The life advice of Polonius – 'neither a borrower nor a lender be' – may or may not be sage, but it comes from an old windbag; the winter of our discontent is only made glorious summer if you subscribe to the self-advertisement of the aspiring tyrant Richard III. 'Our reading is mendicant and sycophantic', writes Emerson in his great essay on 'Self-Reliance' (1841); 'our imagination makes fools of us, plays us false.' We have to learn to sift the bad from the good, the better from the best. We have to learn to discriminate.

Such, of course, is the task of the critic. But it is also the task of the human. Just as good parents should encourage their children to fend for themselves, so good critics should encourage readers to think for themselves. In the end, this is worth more than even the greatest *idée reçue*. 'A man should learn to detect and watch that gleam of light which flashes across his mind from within, more than the lustre of the firmament of bards and sages.' Emerson's advice, were it not so ironically self-defeating, could improve us all. 'In every work of genius we recognise our own rejected thoughts: they come back to us with a certain alienated majesty. Great works of art have no more affecting lesson for us than this.'

Navigating the space between our own ideas and those of others – creating a space *for* our own ideas alongside those of others – is the great challenge of the life of the mind. For what Emerson doesn't say (we might suggest by way of taking him at his word and trusting 'the integrity of our own mind') is that it's far from clear what it even means to have your own ideas. Every idea comes from somewhere, which mostly will mean from elsewhere: in every work of our own we recognize someone else's rejected thoughts. That little word 'own' is nothing if not porous, mixing memory and desire, stirring our own roots with others' rain. Even its grammatical status – is it an adjective, is it a possessive pronoun? – indicates the intermediary nature of our 'own' thoughts. There is nothing immaculate about any of our conceptions.

To try to think for ourselves is to realise that it is impossible to think *by* ourselves; we are always thinking with and against others. The sun shone, having no alternative, on the nothing new: even in having this thought, my Tourette's twitch keeps pointing me elsewhere, to Eliot or Beckett, to Kleist or Emerson. How do we resist being colonised, rather than cultivated, by the ideas of others? The answer, I think, is in (the grammar of) the question: we must push back against passivity. It is certainly necessary to receive the ideas of others, but it is not sufficient; we must make them our own. The standard editorial injunction to use the active voice, to avoid the passive, is as existential as it is stylistic, since it implies an assertion of identity and sensibility – to be active is to be alive. To the feminist imperative to 'lean in', and the psychological imperative to 'nudge', we can add the intellectual imperative to push back. The advice is as timeless as it is timely.

For what *is* purposiveness, if not this? From the moment we are born we are pushing back against existence; until the moment we die we are pushing back against extinction. To think for ourselves, to reject mere contingency, to transcend our historical and geographical circumstances: this is the very essence of human intelligence. If our animal condition is passivity – the parameters of mortal life that are out of our control – our human condition is activity. The more active we can be, the more we propose and pursue our own projects, the more purpose we accrue.

This is another way of saying that work is what defines us – not in the worthy Weberian sense of Protestant piety, but in the broader metaphysical sense that we are always working *towards* something. Work is an aesthetic, as well as an ethic: time-bound creatures, we either move forwards or we are moved forwards. It is for this reason that art can be so obsessive. Creativity is a tyrant, demanding ever-greater offerings on the altar of our own self-image. Perhaps we also need to push back, then, against the hold that the imagination has over us. Do we read, do we write, not to fulfil our fantasies but to *free* ourselves from them? To paraphrase James Joyce, is art a dream from which we are trying to awake? To write is to forget, claims Pessoa; perhaps this is what Walter Benjamin was trying to do with his famous dream of producing a book consisting entirely of quotations – to *get rid* of all those invading thoughts, not gather them. Perhaps, indeed, this is what I am trying to do in writing this book – to write my way *out of* literature, scratched to opacity as it has long since become. To know our mind may also mean to slow our mind.

> *'Do we read, do we write, not to fulfil*
> *our fantasies but to* free *ourselves from them?'*

Imagine, after all, trying to reverse the terms of Benjamin's conceit. What would a book consisting entirely of one's *own* thoughts look like? Taken strictly, it's impossible even to conceive such an undertaking. As we can see from the various names cited in the preceding paragraph, the very idea is prompted by other people's interventions. All we can do is push back against an existing consensus, in the hope that we may make some modest alteration to it. It's a question of degree, not of purity; our own thoughts are always also (at least partially) those of others. To take the emblematic example of humanist self-exploration, Montaigne's *Essais* are littered with references to classical predecessors. To philosophise is to learn how to cite, as well as how to die.

To put it differently, thinking for ourselves is nothing if not a relative concept. To do so, we have to take the slogan at its word and push back against its cognitive presumption. The philosopher Bernard Williams once argued for the merits of what he called 'partial scepticism'. It is (too) easy to be completely sceptical and declare that we know nothing about others' minds, he contended; it is much harder, and much more disturbing, to reflect that we may know something about them, just not exactly what. The same is true, I would suggest, of our intellectual autonomy: we *think* we think for ourselves, we just don't know to what extent. Even for the most forthright among us, partial autonomy is the best we can hope for.

This is equally true, we can now see, of the way we lead our lives. My purpose can never be entirely distinct from yours; my sense of meaning is defined, if only negatively, by other people's. We are all interdependent, however much our sense of pride may want to tell us otherwise. This is why our final commandment, to forget everything you have read, calls us to respect the limits of literature. Life is more than the sum of its arts; there comes a time when even the most bookish among us must learn to put aside bookish things. What was I thinking, obsessively reading Chateaubriand rather than spending time with my wife and children? Why did I suppose that greater meaning and purpose could be found on a page than on a beach? Thinking for ourselves means setting our own priorities and not following those of others – but it also means acknowledging the claims, and the qualities, of others. As the critic Gabriel Josipovici writes of Dante's arrival in heaven, 'joy in paradise comes with recognizing that there are other lives than your own, and it always comes with the sense of purposeful as opposed to purposeless motion'.

*'The ultimate act of independence is
to abjure independence.'*

We have come full circle to our first commandment, only this time with others. As literature teaches us, our purpose is not just our own. Inscribed in the Empyrean, the highest reach of heaven fretted with fire, the ultimate act of independence is to abjure independence. E.M. Forster's famous imperative remains as resonant today as it was in 1910: 'Only connect! That was her whole sermon. Only connect the prose and the passion, and both will be exalted, and human love will be seen at its height. Live in fragments no longer.' That the advice is given by the half-German, intellectually adventurous Margaret Schlegel to the half-witted, intellectually timorous Henry Wilcox underlines the role that the imagination can play in forming us; that the advice is not taken underlines its limits. Thinking for ourselves does not, in the end, mean thinking *by* ourselves. It means seeing ourselves as part of a greater whole. It means connecting the dots between

Figure 10: Joy in paradise:
Gustave Doré, *Paradiso Canto 31*

art and existence, life and literature in such a way that we invest them with, and reflect on, the meaning of creation. Thinking for ourselves, in the final analysis, means thinking on purpose.

EPILOGUE

TEN COMMANDMENTS, ten imperatives: such is the logic of the 'lesson'. If literature teaches us anything, however, it is that we cannot rely on lessons. There is no point in simply lecturing each other. We have to imagine, if not experience, things for ourselves; we have to imagine, if not experience, the meaning of our own lives. The life of the mind can broaden our minds, but it cannot make them up, in any of the several senses of that resonant phrase. We have to make up our own minds; we have to invent, and take responsibility for, our own decisions. My ten imperatives are really ten 'imaginatives', inviting you to consider what *it would mean* to change your mind or be happy, to shape the future or be vulnerable. What would it mean to live 'on purpose'?

The preposition offers various answers. We can think *about* purpose – the classic posture of the essay since Montaigne, pursued through innumerable successors. We can think *with* purpose, which is to say deliberately, consciously, intentionally. But we can also learn to think *without* purpose – as we have seen, this is Kant's seminal view of the function of art.

'Purposiveness without purpose': it is not interest but disinterest that defines artistic experience, understood as a way of guarding against *too much* (self-) interest. Such disinterest lies at the heart, in turn, of aesthetic education. Through learning how to appreciate art dispassionately, we learn how to appreciate our own lives dispassionately. The Kierkegaardian 'either/or' – *either* the aesthetic life, *or* the ethical life – can become a Kantian 'both/and'. Art can make us less self-centred.

But do we even want this? Do we want to live dispassionately? Do we – should we – not want to be the centre of our own lives? To pursue the life of the mind is necessarily to pursue the life of *my* mind. Disinterest, to this extent, is always also interested. The moral imperative to privilege others over the self runs up against the basic fact of partiality, the basic truth that in terms of direct experience, we only have access to our own part of the wider world. *In*directly, however, we contain multitudes: the multitudes of the imagination. Reading can help us to situate ourselves, to expand our native sensibility. Writing can help us to compose ourselves, in both senses of the verb. The challenge, the trick of a lifetime, is to find a balance between my mind and yours, between the inevitable ego and what the Nobel prize-winning poet Louise Glück calls the 'cold, exacting fires of disinterestedness'. The challenge is not so much to repress the self as to refine it.

Literature is as good a refinery as any. Not because it tells us how we should live, but because it shows us how others imagine they might want to live. At its most basic level, literature consists of words, and words offer meaning. Beyond their utilitarian value, beyond even their relationship to each other, words are worlds in miniature, windows onto our common past, our contested present, our uncertain future. With sufficient scrutiny, even random adjectives – *luminous, sheepish, incandescent* – can become one-word poems, flush with their own agenda. Repeat them often enough and they begin to resonate; hold them up to the light and they begin to shine. Their sound, their shape, their un/stressed syllables: whole histories of meaning shimmer through them, through etymologies both physical and metaphysical. Words, to para-phrase Milton's iconic oxymoron, make absence visible. They conjure up something that isn't there, they whisper sweet somethings into our avid ears. Reading, writing, teaching lit-erature enables us to learn how to be attentive to this absent presence. Close attention to the texture of language shows us a microcosm of meaning; close attention to the texture of life, to its stressed and unstressed syllables, can do the same.

Show, don't tell: we have been on this ride before, circling around the commandment on numerous occasions over the course of these ten essays. The advice is as valid for life as it is for literature. My eldest son, with all the accumulated wisdom of his twelve years, often tells me that he doesn't want to hear any 'lessons' from me; he wants, of course, to make his own mistakes. The same is true for all of us. I have suggested ten maxims of meaning, but I am under no illusions that I can always live up to them. If anything, it is *because* I can't always live up to them that they strike me as important and advisable. The things that we are bad at – which includes, in my case, a wide range of emotional registers such as connecting with others, sharing my thinking and taking time 'off' – are the things we need to do deliberately. It is because we live by accident that we need to live on purpose.

Admissions of failure are no mere rhetorical concession. For each and every one of us, they are the stuff of daily existence. We all have the weaknesses of our strengths. Utopia is no-place, unattainable; even our successes suck us in, encouraging a myth of self-made manliness. Covid unmade the myth, showing us how much we depend on *us*, how even the most self-sufficient of intellectuals requires human interaction. To paraphrase Leibniz, we are not windowless monads; in our messy, modern, multicultural lives, a crucial part of our post-pandemic purpose is to acknowledge this interconnection. My meaning – your meaning, our meaning – rewrites centuries of stoicism into a simple acknowledgement: we need each other. We are all multi-purpose.

No ending in literature suggests this quite as plangently as the brief epilogue to Tolstoy's *Anna Karenina*. After the searing intensity of Anna's suicide comes the startling decency of Levin's vision – all the more decent for its unapologetic anchoring in the messy, compromised reality of domestic life:

> I shall still get angry with Ivan the coachman in
> the same way, shall dispute in the same way, shall
> inopportunely express my thoughts; there will still
> be a wall between my soul's holy of holies and other

people; even my wife I shall still blame for my own fears and shall repent of it. My reason will still not understand why I pray, but I shall still pray, and my life, my whole life, independently of anything that may happen to me, is every moment of it no longer meaningless as it was before, but has an unquestionable meaning of goodness with which I have the power to invest it.

Where before there was melodrama, Tolstoy now offers mundanity, the minor key to a major life. Levin acknowledges the inevitability of further fear and failure, but sees in his feelings for his son, and in his thwarted feelings for those around him, a reason to invest his daily doings with purpose. The meaning(lessness) of life is also – is it not always? – the meaning of goodness.

The crucial caveat, however, is in Tolstoy's final phrase. We all have the power to invest our lives with meaning; the question is whether we choose to do so. For what literature teaches us, in the end, is not to sit in our bedrooms and read, but to engage with the world: not to turn inwards, but to turn outwards. What literature teaches us is to step back from ourselves and notice things. Good writing is good observation – open, authentic, unprejudiced observation, the ruthless removal of cliché from our modes of expression and existence. It is easy to do this on occasion, as we meet someone, think something, or arrive somewhere for the first time. It is much harder to *keep* doing it, to retain the wet paint of perspective day after day, week after week, year after year. To see the small things, and to keep seeing the small things, to stay fresh as we grow stale: is this what Levin's prayer amounts to? Is this what it means to live on purpose?

There is a limit to how much we can see others, as there is to how much we can see ourselves. There is a limit, even, to how much we can see the point of our own lives. What ultimate purpose can any finite process have? In our secular, spiritually diminished age, most of us do not have a single way of answering this question, since most of us do not pray like Levin. Perhaps, then, we are better advised cultivating purposiveness rather than purpose, a *sense* of purpose rather than the elusive thing itself. Perhaps this is what fiction, finally, can show us: how to feign ourselves into meaning.

As we feel our way ever further into the post-pandemic era, the time is ripe to ponder our own purposiveness. If literature provides a language in which to do so, it also furnishes a framework for the very idea of purpose, defined as the state of having aims or intentions, the ability to posit things implied by the Latin root *propositum*. We create meaning by positing meaning: to read, to write, to think is to imagine a world, be it modest or magnificent, into miraculous being. But so, if we are only bold enough, is to live: at the end of the millennium I decided to focus and lo, focus came unto me. We don't need gods to live; we need guts.

To do something on purpose is to *have* a purpose: meaning, in the final analysis, is self-generating. It is all the more important, then, that we reflect on what it means to mean.

By encouraging us to think and to feel, by rendering our creaturely existence creative, reading and writing can help us pursue this reflection. In the end, though, it is down to us, poor, bare, forked animals that we are, to find our own focus. In the end, we have to make *ourselves* fit for purpose.

'Le vent se lève! . . . Il faut tenter de vivre!'
PAUL VALÉRY

FURTHER READING

PROLOGUE

W.H. Auden, 'September 1, 1939', in *Selected Poems*, ed. Edward Mendelsohn (Faber & Faber, 2010)

Rainer Maria Rilke, *Duino Elegies*, in *Selected Poems*, tr. Susan Ranson & Marielle Sutherland (Oxford UP, 2011)

Franz Kafka, Letter to Oskar Pollak, 27 January 1904, *Letters to Friends, Family, and Editors*, tr. Richard and Clara Winston (Schocken, 1977)

Joan Didion, *The White Album* (4th Estate, 2017)

Percy Bysshe Shelley, 'Defence of Poetry' (1821), in *Selected Poems and Prose*, ed. Jack Donovan and Cian Duffy (Penguin, 2017)

Virginia Woolf, 'The Russian Point of View' (1925), in *The Common Reader* (Vintage, 2003)

LESSON ONE

Imre Kertész, *Fatelessness*, tr. Tim Wilkinson (Vintage, 2004)

David Constantine, 'Pleasure', *Collected Poems* (Bloodaxe, 2004)

Immanuel Kant, *Critique of Judgement*, tr. James Creed Meredith (Oxford World's Classics, 2007)

Friedrich Schiller, *On the Aesthetic Education of Man*, tr. Keith
 Tribe (Penguin Classics, 2016)

John Keats to Fanny Brawne (1820), *Selected Letters*, ed.
 Robert Gittings (Oxford World's Classics, 2002)

John Keats, *Endymion*, in *The Complete Poems*, ed. John
 Barnard (Penguin, 1977)

Carnal Hermeneutics, ed. Richard Kearney and Brian Treanor
 (Fordham University Press, 2015)

Friedrich Nietzsche, Preface to *Daybreak: Thoughts on the
 Prejudices of Morality*, tr. R.J. Hollingdale (Cambridge UP,
 1998)

Charles Baudelaire, 'A Carcass', in *Selected Poems*, tr. Carol
 Clark (Penguin, 1995)

Sigmund Freud, *Civilisation and its Discontents*, tr. David
 McLintock (Penguin Modern Classics, 2002)

Horace, *Ars Poetica* (*c.* 19 BC): https://www.poetryfoundation.
 org/articles/69381/ars-poetica

Rainer Maria Rilke, 'Archaic Torso of Apollo', in *Selected Poems*,
 tr. Susan Ranson & Marielle Sutherland (OUP, 2011)

LESSON TWO

Charles Dickens, *David Copperfield* (Vintage Classics, 2017)

Ralph Waldo Emerson, 'Self-Reliance', in *Selected Essays*
 (Penguin Classics, 1982)

J.W. von Goethe, *The Sorrows of Young Werther*, tr. David
 Constantine (Oxford World's Classics, 2012)

Ritchie Robertson, *The Enlightenment* (Allen Lane, 2020)

Adam Smith, *The Theory of Moral Sentiments* (Cambridge UP,
 2012)

Joan Didion, *The White Album* (4th Estate, 2017)

T.S. Eliot, *The Poems of T.S. Eliot, Volume 1*, ed. Christopher Ricks and Jim McCue (Faber & Faber, 2018)

Hans Vaihinger, *The Philosophy of 'As If'*, tr. C.K. Ogden (Harcourt Brace, 1924)

Herodotus, *Histories*, tr. Robin Waterfield (Oxford World's Classics, 2008)

John Haffenden, *William Empson, Volume 1: Among the Mandarins* (OUP, 2005)

LESSON THREE

George Eliot, *Middlemarch*, ed. Rosemary Ashton (Penguin, 1994)

Adalbert von Chamisso, *Peter Schlemihl*, tr. Leopold von Loewenstein-Wertheim (Oneworld Classics, 2008)

Nicolas Born, *Gedichte* (Suhrkamp, 1990)

Immanuel Kant, *Critique of the Power of Judgement*, tr. Paul Guyer (Cambridge UP, 2000)

Osip Mandelstam, 'About an Interlocutor', *Selected Essays*, tr. Sidney Molas (University of Texas Press, 1977)

Edward Said, *Reflections on Exile and Other Literary and Cultural Essays* (Granta, 2000)

Montesquieu, *Persian Letters*, tr. Margaret Mauldon (Oxford World's Classics, 2008)

Bertolt Brecht, *Brecht on Art and Politics*, ed. Tom Kuhn and Steve Giles (Methuen, 2003)

LESSON FOUR

Samuel Taylor Coleridge, *Coleridge's Notebooks: A Selection*, ed. Seamus Perry (Oxford UP, 2002)

Vladimir Nabokov, *Lectures on Literature* (Harcourt, 2002)

Ezra Pound, 'A Retrospect', *Literary Essays*, ed. T.S. Eliot (Faber & Faber, 1974)

Paul Valéry, *Bad Thoughts and Not so Bad*, tr. Stuart Gilbert, *Collected Works* vol. 14 (Princeton, 1970)

Fernando Pessoa, *The Book of Disquiet*, tr. Richard Zenith (Penguin, 2015)

Charlie Louth, *Rilke: The Life of the Work* (Oxford UP, 2020)

Saint Augustine, *Confessions*, tr. Henry Chadwick (Oxford World's Classics, 2009)

Czesław Miłosz, *The Captive Mind*, tr. Jane Zielonko (Penguin Modern Classics, 2001)

John Keats, *Selected Letters*, ed. Robert Gittings (Oxford UP, 2009)

Barack Obama and Marilynne Robinson, 'A Conversation', *New York Review of Books*, 19 November 2015

Heinrich von Kleist, 'On the Gradual Production of Thoughts Whilst Speaking', *Selected Writings*, tr. David Constantine (J.M. Dent, 1997)

T.S. Eliot, *The Use of Poetry and the Use of Criticism* (Faber & Faber, 1933)

LESSON FIVE

Herman Melville, *Moby-Dick; or, The Whale* (Readers' Digest, 1996)

Rudolf Erich Raspe, *Baron Munchausen's Narrative of his Marvellous Travels and Campaigns in Russia* (1785)

Fernando Pessoa, *The Book of Disquiet*, tr. Richard Zenith (Penguin, 2015)

Samuel Beckett, *Company / Ill Said / Worstword Ho / Stirrings Still* (Faber & Faber, 2009)

Charles Taylor, *The Language Animal* (Harvard UP, 2016)

Matthew Arnold, *Culture and Anarchy and Other Selected Prose* (Penguin Classics, 2015)

Joseph von Eichendorff, 'Divining Rod', *Poems for the Ages*, tr. William Ruleman (Cedar Springs Books, 2019)

R.M. Rilke, *Sonnets to Orpheus/Duino Elegies*, in *Selected Poems*, tr. Susan Ranson & Marielle Sutherland (OUP, 2011)

LESSON SIX

Population Reference Bureau: https://www.prb.org

G.K. Chesterton, *Orthodoxy* (Ch. 4, 'The Ethics of Elfland') (Loman, 2015)

Ezra Pound, *The Spirit of Romance* (London: J.M. Dent, 1910)

T.S. Eliot, 'Tradition and the Individual Talent', *The Sacred Wood* (Methuen, 1920)

John Ashbery, 'The Ecclesiast', in *Selected Poems* (Carcanet, 2002)

John Milton, *Areopagitica and Other Writings*, ed. William Poole (Penguin Classics, 2014)

Friedrich Nietzsche, 'On the Uses and Disadvantages of History for Life', *Untimely Meditations*, tr. R.J. Hollingdale (Cambridge UP, 1997)

Walter Benjamin, 'The Image of Proust', *Illuminations*, tr. Harry Zohn (Bodley Head, 2015)

Charles Baudelaire, *The Painter of Modern Life*, tr. P.E. Charvet (Penguin, 2010)

Paul Valéry, 'The Crisis of the Mind', tr. Denise Folliot and Jackson Mathews, *Collected Works* vol. 10 (Princeton, 1956)

LESSON SEVEN

George Steiner, *Grammars of Creation* (Faber & Faber, 2001)

David Hume, *An Enquiry Concerning Human Understanding* (Oxford World's Classics, 2008)

Timothy Morton, *All Art is Ecological* (Penguin, 2021)

Michel Foucault, *The Order of Things* (Tavistock, 1970)

Georges Perec, *Species of Spaces and Other Pieces*, tr. John Sturrock (Penguin, 2008)

Goethe, *Faust: Part One*, tr. David Luke (Oxford World's Classics, 2008)

Roland Barthes, *Camera Lucida*, tr. Richard Howard (Vintage, 1993)

Dante, *The Divine Comedy*, tr. C.H. Sisson (Oxford World's Classics, 1993)

Dante, *The Divine Comedy*, tr. Allen Mandelbaum (Everyman's Library, 1995)

Primo Levi, *If this is a Man / The Truce*, tr. Stuart Woolf (Penguin, 1979)

Alfred Lord Tennyson, 'Ulysses', in *Selected Poems*, ed. Christopher Ricks (Penguin Classics, 2007)

Henri Bergson, *Time and Free Will*, tr. F.L. Pogson (Dover, 2001)

LESSON EIGHT

Thomas Hobbes, *Leviathan*, ed. Christopher Brooke (Penguin Classics, 1968)

Pascal, *Pensées*, tr. A. Krailsheimer (Penguin Classics, 1995)

Marcus Aurelius, *Meditations*, tr. Martin Hammond (Penguin Classics, 2006)

Emily Dickinson, *The Complete Poems* (Faber & Faber, 2016)

Paul Celan, *The Meridian*, tr. Pierre Joris (Stanford UP, 2011)

John Milton, *Areopagitica and Other Writings*, ed. William Poole (Penguin Classics, 2014)

George Orwell, 'Politics and the English Language', in *Essays* (Penguin Modern Classics, 2000)

Stanley Cavell, 'The Division of Talent', in *Here and There: Sites of Philosophy* (Harvard, 2022)

Bertolt Brecht, *The Collected Poems of Bertolt Brecht*, tr. David Constantine & Tom Kuhn (Liveright, 2018)

LESSON NINE

Max Weber, *The Protestant Ethic and the Spirit of Capitalism*, tr. Peter Baehr and Gordon C. Wells (Penguin Classics, 2002)

Robert Browning, 'Andrea del Sarto', in *Selected Poems*, ed. Daniel Karlin (Penguin Classics, 1989)

Montaigne, 'On Experience', *Essays*, tr. M.A. Screech (Penguin Classics, 1993)

C.P. Cavafy, 'Ithaka', in *The Complete Poems of C.P. Cavafy*, tr. Daniel Mendelsohn (William Collins, 2014)

C.P. Cavafy, *C.P. Cavafy: Collected Poems*, tr. Edmund Keeley and Philip Sherrard (Princeton UP, 1975)

Paul Éluard, *Le dur désir de durer*, tr. Stephen Spender and Frances Cornford (Trianon Press, 1950)

Samuel Beckett, *Company / Ill Seen Ill Said / Worstward Ho / Stirrings Still* (Faber & Faber, 2009)

Pliny the Elder, *Natural History*, tr. John Healey (Penguin Classics, 1991)

Gustave Flaubert, *Selected Letters*, tr. Geoffrey Wall (Penguin Classics, 1997)

George Eliot, *Felix Holt*, ed. Lynda Mugglestone (Penguin Classics, 1995)

LESSON TEN

Ingeborg Bachmann, *Malina*, tr. Philip Boehm (Penguin, 2019)

Rudyard Kipling, 'Surgeons and the Soul', in *A Book of Words* (Wildside Press, 2007)

Virginia Woolf, *The Waves*, ed. Kate Flint (Penguin, 2019)

Heinrich von Kleist, 'On the Gradual Construction of Thoughts whilst Speaking', tr. David Constantine (J.M. Dent, 1997)

Ralph Waldo Emerson, 'Self-Reliance', in *Selected Essays* (Penguin Classics, 1982)

Bernard Williams, 'The Need to be Sceptical', in *Essays and Reviews 1959-2002* (Princeton, 2014)

Gabriel Josipovici, *100 Days* (Little Island Press/Carcanet, 2021)

E.M. Forster, *Howard's End* (Penguin Classics, 2000)

EPILOGUE

Louise Glück, 'Prism', in *Averno* (Penguin, 2006)

Leo Tolstoy, *Anna Karenina*, tr. Louise and Aylmer Maude (Oxford World's Classics, 1995)

PICTURE CREDITS

Figure 1: Francesco Solimena, *Diana and Endymion* (c. 1710).
Photo credit: Archivart/Alamy Stock Photo.

Figure 2: Honoré Daumier, *Don Quixote and the Windmills*
(c. 1850). Photo credit: SJArt/Alamy Stock Photo.

Figure 3: Adelbert von Chamisso, *Peter Schlemihl* (1814).
Photo credit: Heritage Image Partnership Ltd/Alamy Stock
Photo. This artwork has been cropped.

Figure 4: Philippe de Champaigne, *Saint Augustine* (c. 1650).
Photo credit: IanDagnall Computing / Alamy Stock Photo.

Figure 5: Oskar Herrfurth, Baron von Münchhausen.
Photo credit: Gainew Gallery/Alamy Stock Photo.

Figure 6: Nicolas Poussin, *Orion aveugle cherchant le soleil*
(1658). Photo credit: The Picture Art Collection/Alamy
Stock Photo. This artwork has been cropped.

Figure 7: Samuel Palmer, *Calypso's Island, Departure of Ulysses,
or Farewell to Calypso* (1848–9). Photo credit: Whitworth
Art Gallery/Bridgeman Images. This artwork has been
cropped.

Figure 8: Thomas Hobbes, Frontispiece to *Leviathan* (1651).
Photo credit: IanDagnall Computing/Alamy Stock Photo.

Figure 9: Titian, *Annunciation* (c. 1564). Photo credit: Artefact/Alamy Stock Photo.

Figure 10: Gustave Doré, *Paradiso Canto 31*. Photo credit: Darling Archive/Alamy Stock Photo.